Discovering the
WHAT
of management

Discovering the WHAT

of management

The complete guide
to The Kenning Principles
of Management™

Paula K. Martin

Published by Renaissance Educational Services
P.O. Box 1088
Flemington, New Jersey 08822
201-806-3974

Manufactured in the United States of America by
BookCrafters

ISBN: 0 - 943811 - 01 - 5

Dedication

This book is dedicated to George Kenning's wife, Mary, and to his children: Stephanie, George, Kathryn, and Christine.

Acknowledgements

Thanks to:

Joel Weinstein, my husband, for his constant encouragement and for
his literary inputs on the book.
Mary Kenning, George Kenning's wife, for her patience and kind
support during the long process of putting the book together.
Gray Mason, for her copy editing, and for her constant reminders
about the dangers of "comma splices" which will never be forgotten, although continually ignored.
Bob Wilbur, for his help in developing The Principles and for his
guidance on their interpretation.

The Reviewers who provided their honest opinions, both positive and
negative, at various stages of the book process.

> **Valerie Hart**
> **Robert Herrick**
> **Per Arne Holmberg**
> **Georgia Larsen**
> **Meredith Martin**
> **Thorvald Reinertsen**
> **Larry Simms**
> **Frank Tenne**
> **Laura Whatley**

Disclaimer

All characters and companies (except the characters of the consultant, Robert Wilbur and George Kenning) are purely fictitious, and any similarity to companies or people, living or dead, is purely coincidental.

Preface

Discovering the WHAT of management is an explanation of the Kenning Philosophy of Management. I have tried to remain true to the intent of George Kenning's philosophy, but unfortunately, George died before the book was written, so he did not have the opportunity to review the manuscript. However, Bob Wilbur and Thorvald Reinertsen, both long time associates of George's and experts on the interpretation of the Principles, carefully reviewed the book to ensure that it was consistent with George Kenning's thinking on management.

Those familiar with George Kenning's work will notice both minor changes in the wording of some of the Principles and the addition of new Principles. The Kenning Philosophy was originally set down in the form of '31 points' of management, which George called *Praxes*. Before George's death, Bob Wilbur and I sat with George and reconstructed the principles of management from the ground-up, or more accurately, from the concept of the organization to the rules of the manager-to-specialist interaction. The result of that effort is The Kenning

Principles of Management™. There are no new concepts in these Principles, just an expansion of the themes covered in George's earlier '31
points.' Some of the language was changed to make the Princples
more easily understood.

The book was written to be entertaining, yet serious. It was written
to be read from front to back or used as a reference text. It is a book
that, hopefully, you'll want to keep and refer to as a constant reminder
of what management is, really.

I hope that this book will enhance the understanding of The Kenning Principles of Management. They have been an important part of
my management career, and I appreciate the opportunity to share them
with you.

Paula K. Martin
Flemington, New Jersey
February, 1990

Table of Contents

Prologue

The Challenge

1

I was stunned as I closed the door of my boss's office. I couldn't believe what had happened. Everything had changed. I was excited and I was scared. I went back over the events of the morning to assure myself that I wasn't dreaming.

I had been in my office catching up on some paperwork when my boss, the Director of Shipping, called and asked to see me. "Sure," I said, "I'll be right over."

I wondered what she wanted as I walked to her office. I entered her waiting area and noticed a man sitting by her door. I wondered why she had called me if she had another appointment, but her secretary said she was expecting me, to go right on in.

My boss directed me to have a seat on the couch. She sat in the wing chair to my left. This seating arrangement meant that serious discussions were planned. We spent the first five minutes or so discussing my last assignment. With that out of the way, she said she had something of importance to discuss.

"I want to talk to you about your career," she said.

I sat up a little straighter. She had my attention.

She continued, "You've been doing an excellent job here in the Chemicals Division. You've proven yourself to be an excellent ship's captain and a good manager."

It registered immediately that she had said I was only a 'good' manager. I wondered what that meant.

"We think you've got management potential, but you need more experience, and you need to be tested."

"Tested?" I said, trying to figure out what she was getting at.

"Yes. You need to demonstrate that you can manage something other than what you're familiar with. You practically grew up on the ship you're managing now."

"That's true."

"If you can demonstrate that you've got real management talent, which by the way I think you do have, you'll get a shot at higher level positions."

I was amibitious and I had hoped one day to get her job, when she got promoted, of course. However, when you work for a company like Global Enterprises, in which shipping is only a minor part of the operation, how far can a ship's captain expect to go?

She stood up and walked to the window. She surveyed the river below and then turned and said very seriously, "There's no limit to how far you could go if you can sharpen your managerial skills. To do that, you've got to get out of shipping, even though I hate to lose you. Global needs great managers more than it needs great ship captains."

I leaned forward and waited for what would come next.

"As I am sure you are aware," she said, "Global has been expanding its life sciences businesses and contracting its commodity businesses. As part of this expansion, we have started up a new venture, a wholly owned subsidiary, called 'Sea Life Enterprises.' The purpose of this venture is to discover sea organisms with commercially important biological activity. Somehow, through the use of biotechnology, which I must admit I don't understand, those leads will eventually become new products for our medical and agricultural divisions."

Now I was really beginning to wonder where I fit in the picture. I knew nothing about research or biology.

"The person who had been hired as the director of the off-shore part of the operation and who would have captained the research vessel was killed in a car accident a couple of weeks ago. Sea Life has no replacement for him. They need someone who can captain a ship as well as manage a not-so-typical crew. The ship is essentially a floating laboratory, so the crew is a combination of research types, mostly marine biologists, and your typical operational crew. You know the engineers, navigators, cooks, etc."

"But I don't know anything about research."
"Yes, I know, and that was their concern, which is why it took me a while to convince them you were worth talking to. I explained to them that this was a management job, not a research job, and that there'd be a manager of research on the vessel, reporting to you, who would know the research end of things. Besides, you're a fast learner. You'll pick up what you need to know. Hey, I manage the Shipping Operation," she said, "and I'm not a ship's captain."
"That's true." She did a damn good job, too. "This is all quite hard to believe."

"Yes, I'm sure it is," she said, "Let me explain the rest of the situation. The crew has already been chosen. The ship is scheduled for its maiden voyage in two months. It will be on a three months out, one month in, schedule. The venture has been given three years to come up with a significant lead. If you're successful, the company will prosper; the program will continue; you'll have proven you can manage; and Global will consider you for its senior management track."

"And, if I'm not successful?" I hated to ask that question.
"Then you're out of a job. Of course, I'd take you back if I had an opening, but there aren't any guarantees."

Success or unemployment. It sounded like the stakes were high.
"Global is investing a lot of money in this venture. It's risky, but the return could be enormous. All you have to do is manage. What do you say?"
All I have to do is manage. What is management, really? I thought. The next thing I knew I was saying, "I'm interested."

"Good. The President of Sea Life is waiting outside to talk to you. I'll go get him." She left to get the man I had seen on the way in. Everything was happening a little too quickly.

The three of us sat down, and the President started to ask me questions. He asked me about my management career, and he asked me to describe my crew and my last few assignments. I can't remember exactly what I said. I was talking in a daze. I remember describing what I considered to be the outstanding accomplishments of my career. When I finished, I paused, waiting for his next question. He just sat and studied me.

"What makes you think you can do this job?" he asked.
"It sounds like what you need is someone who can captain a ship, which I've demonstrated I can do, and someone who can manage both the operational and research components of the mission. Admittedly, I don't have any experience in research, but I have learned a little something about management over the past ten years. If the people on

the research crew know what they're doing, which I trust they do, then I'm certain I can manage them," I said sounding much more confident that I actually felt.

"I also understand that you're under severe time constraints in terms of making something happen. That isn't any different, really, than the everyday world of business where one constantly has to do things better, faster, and cheaper, or get beat out by the competition. I work well under that kind of pressure, and I like a challenge. That's why you should hire me." Here I was trying to talk him into hiring me, and I wasn't sure I could even do the job. If I failed, I was on the breadline. Was I crazy?

He looked at me and then at my boss. She was smiling. He stood up and put out his hand, "You're hired then. I'm counting on your managerial abilities."

I found myself saying, "Yes, thank you sir."

He turned to my boss and asked, "When can I have him?"

"I'll need some time to identify a replacement. Is four weeks acceptable?"

"Make it three," he said.

She looked at me. I heard myself saying, "No problem."

Now what was I going to do?

The Search   2

It took about a week for the shock to wear off, but the nagging feeling that I wasn't prepared for my new assignment only grew stronger. I felt there was something missing in my understanding of what management was all about, and I decided to try to find out what it was.

I bought a pile of the latest management books and plowed through them searching for an answer. I was told to manage by objectives in one book and not to in another. I was told to be a leader. I was told to focus on quality. I was told many useful things, but somehow they weren't *it*.

I couldn't really describe what I was looking for. It was something fundamental, something at the heart of management, that seemed to be missing. After an MBA and ten years of management experience, I still felt I was managing without a clear map of the territory. I needed that map to succeed in my new job.

I asked some of the more successful managers I knew at Global if they knew what management was fundamentally all about. 'What are the principles that guide the management process?' I would ask. They shook their heads and looked at me like I was Don Quixote chasing windmills. Maybe I was.

I was sitting at home, with just over a week left before I had to report to my new assignment, trying to convince myself that I knew as much about management as everyone else seemed to know, so there was nothing to worry about. Maybe what I was looking for didn't exist.

The ringing of the phone disrupted my thoughts. I debated whether to answer it or not. I wasn't in the mood to talk to someone wanting money. I tossed a coin. Heads I pick it up; tails I let it ring. It was heads. I was relieved to hear the voice of one of my old MBA friends on the other end. I hadn't heard from her in years.

"How are things going?" I asked.
"Terrific. Guess what?"
"What?"
"I got promoted. They've made me President and CEO of Lanxica."
"No kidding!" I said, "that's fantastic!"
"Yea, I'm really stunned. I still can't believe it. Of course, I was the best candidate and I deserve the job."
"Of course."
"If they had promoted someone else it would have been a terrible mistake."
"Of course."
She laughed and said, "I had to call you. You remember how we used to talk about making it to the top? Of course, Lanxica isn't that big, not anything like Global, but it's a start. Speaking of Global, how are things going with you? Still sailing the deep, blue sea?"

I told her about my new assignment and my search to find the answer to the question of what management was really all about. I asked if she had any ideas on the subject.

"I do indeed," she said. "I have exactly what you need."

"You do?" I said excitedly.

"Yes. I discovered the fundamentals of management several years ago. I think they've been the most significant factor in my managerial success."

"Really? What are they?"

"They're called The Kenning Principles of Management."

"The WHAT?"

"The Kenning Principles. A kind of constitution of management. They are the Principles that guide the management process. Most of the stuff they taught us in school described the *how-to's* of management. The Kenning Principles describe the *what* of management."

"That's it! That's what I've been looking for. Do you have a book or something I can read?"

"No. But, I can give the number of a consultant who teaches the Principles. She gives a course called 'Back to Basics.' I think she has one coming up in a month or two."

"A month! I need something now! What's her number?"

"Just a minute, I'll get it." She gave me the number and wished me luck. I remembered to wish her luck, as well, before I hung up.

It was past 7 p.m. by this time, but I decided to call anyway. As expected, I got a machine. I left a message and waited for the morning.

I called first thing the next morning and got connected to the consultant immediately. I explained that my friend from Lanxica had given me the number, and that I was interested in learning the principles of management.

"Great," she said. "I have a course coming up. Let me look at the schedule here..."

"You don't understand. I'm starting my new assignment in a week and a half."

She asked me to explain my new assignment. When I had finished she said, "I want to be sure you understand that although The Kenning Principles will help you become a better manager, they cannot ensure that you'll be successful at finding new products. Whether or not you're successful in accomplishing that goal will depend on a number of factors, such as the strategy you have for finding the organisms, the expertise of your crew, the methods you use to screen the organisms, not to mention plain, old-fashioned, luck.

"What the Principles *can* do for you is help you create an organization that works together, where everyone is headed in the same direction. They can provide a common management language and a set of operating rules for the management of your organization. Of course, these factors will help you reach your goal, because the more effectively your ship operates as a unit, the better your chances of finding new products."

"I wasn't looking for guarantees," I said. "I know that success is a combination of factors, one of which is having a firm foundation in the management process. Is there any way I could learn these Principles before I start my new job?" I waited for an answer.

"Well," she said, "I think I could find some time next week to teach you the Principles, if you can to come to my office."

"I'll be there. What day do we start?"

We agreed to meet the first thing Tuesday morning.

Day One

Organizations

3

The consultant took my coat, handed me a notebook and a notepad, and showed me to my seat.

"No sense wasting time with preliminaries," she said, "we only have three days, so we'd better get right to work. Would you like a cup of coffee?"

"Yes. Black. Thanks, " I said as I quickly pulled a pen from my jacket pocket and sat down.

"Are you ready to get started?" she asked, seating herself comfortably.

"Ready," I answered.

"Good. Let me give you an overview of the Kenning Principles."

I had been looking forward to finding out what the Principles were really all about.

"The Principles," she said, "are about the underlying fundamentals of the management process. They address the *what* of management: what is management, what is the role of the manager, what are the rules of management. The *what* is different from the *how*. The *how* addresses the skills or techniques needed to effectuate the management process, but before you can be effective using the *how*, you need to know *how to do what*. The Kenning Principles tell you what managers are supposed to do."

"This sounds like the famous Abbott and Costello skit," I said chuckling.

"I guess it does. Another point I want to cover is that the Principles address what *can and should be*, not what *is*. All managers have stored in their brains a picture of what management means to them. This picture is based on the individual's education and experience. Each individual's understanding or picture of *management as it is in the real world* is valid. The Kenning Principles provide an alternate picture: *management as it can and should be*. The Principles describe how management should operate, not necessarily how management operates now. Let me illustrate this for you."

She got up and walked over to a flip chart that stood on the opposite side of the room. She picked up one of the black magic markers and began to draw.

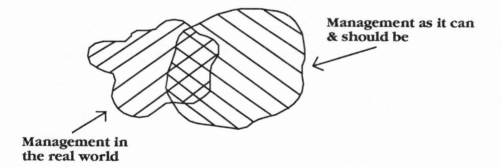

Management as it can
& should be

Management in
the real world

"On the left is one manager's picture of management in the real world. On the right is a picture of management as it can and should be which is also called management according to the Kenning Principles. As you see, the two pictures overlap. That means that some of the

Principles we'll discuss will probably fit with your own ideas about management. On the other hand, some of the Principles will probably differ from your ideas about management. My job for the next three days is to help you understand the picture of management as it can and should be, the picture of the Kenning Principles. Whether or not you choose to implement the Principles when you return to Global is, of course, entirely up to you." She sat down.

"That sounds reasonable," I said.

"We will be developing the Principles from scratch, concept by concept. Hopefully, you've come prepared to do some thinking?"

"It's one of my strengths," I replied.

"Good. Here is the schedule for the next three days. Today we'll cover some of the basics: organizations, organizational structure, accountability, responsibility and organizational accountability. To-morrow we'll cover the role of the manager, criteria for managers, line relationships and staff relationships. On the third day we'll cover the role of the specialist, manager-to-specialist relationships, manager-to-manager relationships and manager development. We'll finish the third day by going back to some organizational concepts. Are you ready to get started?"

"Ready," I replied as I sipped my cup of hot coffee. I felt a strange mixture of relaxation and excitement.

"We'll begin with the foundation of the Principles, and that founda-tion is an understanding of the basic characteristics of an organization. Why are organizations formed in the first place? Let's say you're an entrepreneur, working by yourself. What would prompt you to form an organization?"

I thought about the question for a minute and then responded, "Be-cause I need help."

"Help to do what?"

"To accomplish my goals."

"Right. An organization exists to accomplish something, to get something done, to go somewhere. An organization is needed when what needs to be accomplished, the goal or goals, cannot be accomplished by just one person or even a small group of people."

That seemed obvious to me.

"Do you have an organization?" she asked.

"I guess you could say my crew is my organization."

"Why do you need a crew?"

"Well, I couldn't run a ship without one. I couldn't transport cargo around the world without help. I certainly couldn't discover new products without help. Essentially, I couldn't accomplish my goals without a crew."

"Can you think of a goal that wouldn't require a crew?"

"Well, I could run a small cargo operation on a small river. I could do all the bookings, the loading and unloading, the navigation, etc."

"So, the goal of transporting cargo on a small river doesn't require an organization, but the goal of discovering new products or transporting cargo around the world does. It's the goal that determines your need for an organization. You don't form an organization first, and then wonder where you want to go. You form an organization to reach a goal that could not be reached without one. The goal is the reason for the existence of the organization. She flipped to the next page on the flip chart and started writing.

Characteristics of an Organization:

* Common goal

She continued with her explanation, "The goals that an organization can accomplish are larger and more complex than the goals an individual can accomplish. That is why the more advanced a society becomes, the more organizations it seems to have."

It did seem like everywhere you looked there were organizations. I'd never thought much about why that was before.

"We've established that you need help in order to reach your goal. You can't do all the tasks on the ship yourself."

"Not only can't I physically do them all, I don't even know *how* to do them all."

"So not all tasks are the same?"

"No. There are engineering tasks, navigational tasks, maintenance tasks, etc."

"Not only do you need people, but you need people with specialized skills?"

"Exactly."

"You've just arrived at the second characteristic of an organization: specialization."

Characteristics of an Organization:

* Common goal

* Specialization

"Let's examine a theoretical company, the XYZ Company, for a minute. XYZ has the goal of becoming the largest supplier of widgets in the world. This is a complex goal and it requires an organization. The head of the XYZ Company has decided she needs specialized help in five areas: engineering, manufacturing, administration, sales and marketing. She has grouped similar specialities or activities together, such as the engineering group, the manufacturing group, etc. Each of these groups is given a piece of the common goal. What would happen if the manufacturing group did not fulfill its part of the goal?"

"The company would be in trouble. You've got to have something to sell."

"What if sales didn't sell?"

"Then the company would go under."

"What if engineering didn't design the right widgets?"

"Again, no sales."

"That means that when you divide up the whole, the common goal, into parts, each part depends on every other part to take care of its piece of the goal. Otherwise, the organization suffers. This interdependence is a result of specialization."

Characteristics of an Organization:

* Common goal

* Specialization

* Interdependence

She went on to explain that everyone on the ship is there to contribute to the common goal. Everyone has been given a piece of the overall goal to accomplish and if any piece does not get done and get done properly, then the organization's ability to reach its goal will be impeded. The cook relies on the engineer to take care of his piece of the work burden and vice versa. If the cook fails, the engineer could starve. If the engineer fails, the cook could be stranded at sea. Each member of the organization is dependent on the other members of the organization to do their part in keeping the ship afloat.

"How does an individual benefit from specialization?" she asked.

"The individual doesn't have to do all the tasks himself. He can contribute his own specialty to the organization."

"Right. The individual does not have to be a jack of all trades. If his specialty is accounting, he can concentrate on doing accounting. Specialization does not mean we break each activity down into its most robotic function. It merely means we group activities together and then try to match those groups of activities, which are called a job, to someone with the appropriate specialized abilities or skills. This utilizes the strengths of the individual. If you focus those individual strengths on a common goal, you have a very powerful organization."

"That's exactly what I'm looking for," I said.

"It's not as easy as it sounds," she replied.

Of course I knew that. Otherwise, I wouldn't be sitting in her conference room trying to figure out the secrets to creating a powerful organization.

"Aren't there disadvantages to specialization?" I asked.

"Such as?"

"The individual can become a cog in the wheel and lose his feeling of contributing to the whole."

"That's certainly a real danger, and we'll need to keep that in mind as we talk about management in more depth later.

"Based on our discussions so far, how would you define an organization?" she asked.

"It's a group of interdependent people with specialized skills, working toward a common goal," I said smugly.

"Close."

**An organization is a formal entity, consisting of
an interdependent group of people, working
together, under direction, toward a common goal.**

I copied the definition into my notebook while she continued,
"There are two concepts in the definition we haven't yet covered.
First, an organization is a formal entity, not a loosely associated group
of people. In a way, an organization is alive. It's an organism of sorts,
and it wants to stay alive. It is also something you can identify, something you can name, like Metropolitan General Hospital or the Bureau
of Indian Affairs or Global Enterprises.

"The other concept we need to cover is direction. Imagine the
organization as a ship. What would the result be if there were no direction?"

"The ship would go around in circles," I replied.

"Right. Direction is critical to ensure that the organization stays on
course towards its goal."

Characteristics of an Organization:

* **Common goal**

* **Specialization**

* **Interdependence**

* **Formal entity**

* **Under direction**

I thought about the basic characteristics of an organization while the consultant excused herself to answer a phone call. There was nothing new in the definition, but it held new implications for me. I hadn't given the importance of interdependence much thought before.

She returned from her phone call and said, "We need to cover the two basic roles within an organization."

"Managers and nonmanagers?" I volunteered.

"Right, but we're going to call nonmanagers, specialists. The reason for this should be obvious in a minute. What is the role of the specialist in the organization?"

"They do the tasks."

"Exactly. They are the people who perform the specialized tasks or activities in an organization. They are the doers: the crew members, the engineers, the radio operators, the deck hands. They perform the work of the ship. They run the engines; they chart the course; they swab the decks. They are the producers in an organization. Without specialists to perform the work, your ship would never move."

"Are you saying managers don't work?" I asked.

"No, but I'm using the word 'work' to mean the specialized tasks or activities that move the organization toward its goal. That is why we call nonmanagers 'specialists,' because they do the specialized work of an organization. What managers do is something different. They coordinate and direct the work. They bring order to the chaos. They make sure the work being done is consistent with attaining the goals of the organization. The specialists do the tasks; the managers direct the tasks."

"I'm a manager and I do tasks."

"The tasks managers do relate to coordinating and directing the work of others. If they are doing the actual *work*, themselves they are acting as specialists, not managers."

I considered the differences in tasks as she had described them. Manager tasks involved planning, controlling, budgeting, reporting, etc., whereas specialist tasks involved producing, moving, selling, fixing, etc. I decided she was right. The manager's tasks weren't really work; they were part of getting the *work* done.

"What would happen if you removed all the specialists from your organization?" she asked.
"If you did that nothing would happen. The ship wouldn't move."
"What if you removed all the managers instead?"
"The ship might move but it wouldn't get anywhere."

"Exactly. Both groups, working together, are needed for the organization to reach its goal, but each group has a unique role. The specialists do the work, and the managers direct the work."

Specialists = workers

Managers = directors

She summarized what we had covered by saying that an organization is a group of people, working together toward a common goal. Some of the people in the organization do the work of the organization and are called specialists. Other people in the organization direct the resources of the organization, and they are called managers. Both groups are equally important to the health and vitality of the organization. Finally, all members of the organization are interdependent.

Organizational Principles

4

The first session prompted me to think about an organization's need for a common set of principles or rules. A football team was an organization. What would happen if they didn't have a common set of rules? The result would be chaos. A management team also needs a common set of rules. Maybe that was part of our problem at Global. Everyone was playing by different rules even though we were all trying to cross the same goal line.

The consultant snapped me out of my contemplation, "Are you ready to move on, or would you prefer to daydream all day? It's the same to me. I get paid either way."

"I can't afford to have you watch me daydream. Let's move on," I replied.

"The next topic is Organizational Principles. I will give you a Principle. Then I want you to explain to me why that Principle makes sense based on what we have talked about so far. This is a test of your inductive reasoning. Ready?"

"Fire."

Organizational Principle No. 1: **All members of an organization must act for the organizational good. Therefore, an individual must not succeed at the expense of the organization.**

I considered the Principle and said, "The first part seems self-evident. Since everyone is working toward the common goal, everyone is therefore acting for the common good. The second part is trickier. An individual must not succeed at the expense of the organization. I think the words, 'at the expense of,' are key here. It doesn't say an individual cannot succeed. It says he can't put his own success ahead of the success of the organization, because everyone is dependent on the organization's success. If an individual succeeds at the expense of the whole, then everyone in the organization suffers."

"And, in the end," she explained, "the individual who succeeded at the expense of the organization will also suffer since he too is dependent on the organization. Of course you want successful individuals within an organization, but every individual must keep in mind that he belongs to an organization for the specific purpose of contributing to the success of the whole, not for his own personal gain."

I thought about the managers I knew at Global who tried to succeed at the expense of the organization, like Joe Dogbane. Joe is a political guy who only cares about his own success. People hate to work *for* Joe. People hate to work *with* Joe. I wondered why Joe's behavior is so offensive to most people. I thought interdependence might have something to do with it. Joe had betrayed his commitment to the organization. He had sacrificed the common good for his own individual good. As a result, people had stopped trusting Joe.

"Try the next Principle," she said.

Organizational Principle No. 2: Organizational functioning is the result of each member of the organization fulfilling his or her role within the organization. Every member of an organization is equally important.

"It seems obvious," I said, "that if the common goal is broken down into its component pieces and if everyone is given a piece of the goal to take care of, then the organization functions effectively only when everyone does what he is assigned to do, or when he fulfills his role within the organization." I paused trying to make some sense out of the second sentence. 'Every member of an organization is equally important.' How could that be? "I'm sorry. I can't accept the second half of that Principle. It's just not true that every member of the organization is equally important. Some people are paid more than others, and I think they should be."

"You're confusing value and importance. As you said, all members of an organization have a part of the common goal to take care of: it is called their job. If a job isn't needed to achieve the common goal, then it shouldn't exist. It should be eliminated. If you have an extra cook on your ship who you don't need, that's a burden to the ship with no benefit."

"Are you saying get rid of the dead wood?"

"Exactly. If a job exists, then the organization must need that job to reach its goal, and, therefore, the person doing that job must be important to the organization. Every member of the organization is equally important because every job is needed for the organization to reach its goals. People are doing different jobs, but that does not mean one person is more important than another."

"Are you saying everyone should receive equal pay?" I asked.

"No, not every member of the organization is of equal value to the organization, so not everyone will be paid the same. Market supply and demand, skill levels, individual talents, etc. will determine the value placed on an individual in a particular job. But, every member of the organization is an equally important part of the whole."

"I guess if you differentiate value and importance, I can see that all the members of an organization are important - they are simply doing different jobs."

"Right."

Organizational Principle No. 3: Organizational efficiency is produced through units working together interdependently and cohesively. An organization is only as good as its least effective unit.

"What is a unit?" I asked.

"In a small organization, the unit would be the individual. In a larger organization, a unit might be a section or a department."

"Okay. " I said, "Let's suppose the accounting section is outstanding, but if it doesn't cooperate with the other units in the organization, what good is it to the organization? I'm speaking from experience here. It is amazing how one section, particularly a support or service section, can drag everyone else down. This is the concept of interdependence again."

"Since everyone depends on everyone else," she said, "it doesn't have to be just a service or support section that pulls down the rest of the organization. In fact, any weak section pulls everyone else down. If engineering designs lousy widgets, everyone suffers. If manufacturing makes defective widgets, everyone suffers."

"I guess you're right."

> **Organizational Principle No. 4**: As an entity, an organization does not make decisions, but does provide a framework within which decisions can be made in an orderly manner.

"This is a little more difficult," I said. "I guess this means that individuals, not organizations, make decisions. It also seems to say that one should know where within an organization a decision should be made."

"Right. The framework provided by an organization which facilitates orderly decision making is called the organizational structure. One purpose of the structure is to identify where decisions should be made. It is important for members of an organization to know who is supposed to make what level of decision."

"If only individuals make decisions," I asked, "what about committees or decisions by consensus?"

"Decisions by committee or consensus lead to stagnation, inertia and confusion. A decision must be made by an individual. He might solicit inputs before making a decision. He might even use a commit-tee to get those inputs, but ultimately the individual must make a decision, not a committee."

"Do specialists make decisions under the Kenning Principles?"

"Of course. The specialist decision usually concerns itself with how-to-do something. The manager is usually making decisions related to what-to-do. This leads to the next Principle."

Organizational Principle No. 5: Decisions should be made at the lowest level possible.

I immediately identified with this Principle because I had worked for a captain once who insisted on making every decision. I said, "A captain, for example, doesn't need to decide what temperature to cook the eggs for breakfast. He doesn't need to decide how to repair the engines. If decisions are pushed down, then the person with the most complete information can make the decision. It's going to depend on the decision as to how far down it needs to go."

"That's correct. What this Principle says is that there is value in making decisions at the lowest level possible, and you're right - get it down to where the information is. If it's a decision about how to do a task, then the appropriate level might be the specialist level. If it's a strategic decision, then it will be at a managerial level. What we don't want happening is to have the third or fourth level of management making decisions that a first line manager should make."

"It happens all the time," I said.

"Unfortunately, you're right."

I thought about the effect of making decisions at too high a level. I remembered how useless I had felt when I had worked for the captain who decided everything himself. I had felt my only role in that operation was as a messenger, to pass along his decisions. I resolved to work harder at not making the same mistake myself.

"Well," she said, "that completes the first installment of the Principles. Are you learning anything?"

"Definitely. The Principles seem like common sense, but they're not quite as simple as they sound. What comes next?"

"Organizational structure."

Organizational Structure

5

"The structure of an organization is like the lay-out of a house," she explained. "A house is laid-out by rooms and the lay-out is depicted by a map or floor plan of the house. The floor plan is not the house itself, but a picture of how the house is laid-out. An organizational structure is the lay-out of the organization, and it is pictured by an organizational chart or model. The chart tells you where to find the 'rooms' of the organization.

"A floor plan will help you locate the rooms of the house, but it cannot tell you how the house is run. It can't tell you if there is a loose, casual attitude about the management of the household or a tight, authoritarian management style. It merely tells you where the rooms are. Similarly, an organizational chart cannot tell you what management style an organization has. It merely provides a map of an organization that can help you get around."

"Like a road map?" I asked.
"Exactly. Let's discuss the XYZ Company again. We divided the overall goal up among specialty groups, which I call functions. Now

let's draw up an organizational chart for XYZ. We'll look at the sales function in detail." Almost instantly a system of boxes and circles appeared on the flip chart.

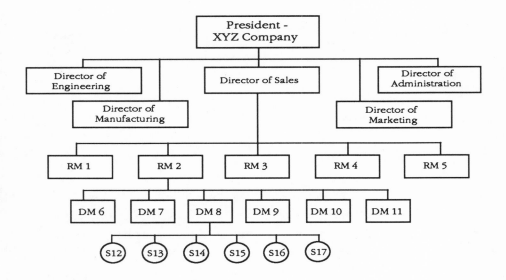

"Each of the boxes represents a manager's area of activity. That's the area he directs. RM means regional manager. DM means district manager. Each of the circles represents a salesperson."

"What value is there in having an organizational chart?" I asked.

"For one, it serves to tell you who has what resources. An organization is a resource bank. The organizational chart tells you how the resources are divided up and where to go to get some help from resources in another part of the bank. It also tells you who reports to whom. For example, I can tell that salesperson 16 reports to district manager 8 who reports to regional manager 2 who reports to the sales director who reports to the president."

"This all sounds like a very traditional hierarchical structure. Isn't that out of vogue? Isn't it the rage to have no structure at all or a loose structure?" I asked.

"The traditional structure of an organization has been under attack. It is claimed that the traditional structure, like the one depicted in the XYZ diagram, represents an authoritarian, top-down management style. How authority flows within an organization cannot be surmised from the organizational chart or map, just as the style of household management cannot be determined from the floor plan of a house. In fact, a very flat chart, which seems to be popular today, is no more bottom-up than a pyramidal chart. The opposite could be true. In a flat structure, managers have lots of people reporting to them. When a manager has a lot of subordinates, he might have to use a more authoritarian style to get things done because he has much less time to spend with each subordinate. A manager with fewer subordinates should have more time to solicit inputs from his subordinates, making his a more bottom-up organization.

"The nature of the decision making process in an organization is not determined by the structure. The structure merely tells you where certain kinds of work are done and where decisions should be made."

"That makes sense," I replied.

"Now let's look at some Organizational Structure Principles."

Organizational Structure Principle No. 1: An organizational structure provides for an orderly division of the work burden.

I struggled for a minute, then gave it a try, "I guess the work burden is the sum total of what needs to get done in order to reach the goal. The whole is divided up into groups of specialties or functions and then divided again and again until you get to the smallest chunk you can have, the unit of work for one individual, the specialist."

"That was excellent," she said. "Here's another easy one for you."

> ### Organizational Structure Principle No. 2:
> **Organizations should be structured to fulfill the organizational mission. First, functions (groups of related activities) required to fulfill the mission should be determined. Then, the activities within each function should be defined.**

"The purpose of having an organization is to do something, to fulfill a goal or a mission. An organization should be organized or structured to most effectively fulfill that mission."

"Right, again. There's no one perfect structure. It depends on what the organization wants to accomplish and how it decides to divide up the accountabilities. For example, if you wanted to structure a new law firm, you would first determine your mission. Let's say it is to provide a complete line of legal services to the public. Then you would look at what functions were needed to fulfill that mission. Accounting might be one, sales/advertising might be another, operations would be the legal function itself, and legal support might be another function. Each function is composed of related activities. Within accounting the activities might be accounts payable, accounts receivable, general ledger entry, etc. Within legal support the activities might be research, documentation, transcription, etc. By determining the mission, then the function, and then activities, you start with the whole and then break it down into smaller and smaller parts. In that way, you ensure that the mission of the organization stays in focus and does not get lost in the details. The organizational structure reflects the division of the work."

"What if you already have an organization and your mission changes? What do you do then?"

"You begin by thinking about your structure as if you were starting from scratch and didn't have an existing structure at all. Forget what you've already got. First determine what functions you need to accomplish your new mission. That will force you to rethink the organizational structure in terms of what is needed for the future, not by what is dictated from the past. After you've redrawn the structure, determine if the people you have fit into the new structure. The temptation is, of course, to restructure around the people you've got, but that is the wrong thing to do."

"Won't you have to make some compromises in the structure based on the people you've got?"

"Let's take that up in the next Principle."

Organizational Structure Principle No. 3: Organizations should not be structured around individual capacities or needs.

I tried to explain this Principle. "This relates to what you just said and to the Principle that the individual cannot succeed at the expense of the organization. An organization shouldn't be structured to satisfy the needs of the individual over the needs of the organization."

"Exactly. Although there must be a meshing of organizational and individual needs, the organizational interests must come first. An organization should not be structured based on individual needs.

"Suppose you work for the ABC Company and you're the boss of a manager named Jack. Although Jack was a good manager at one time, he is no longer effective. He's put in a lot of time with the company; he's loyal, a nice guy, and he loves the organization. And, he has family problems. For the good of the organization, you have to move Jack out of his present position. Of course, that means you have failed with Jack, but you can't leave him where he is. You have given him a fair shot, taken into account his personal problems, but he just doesn't cut the mustard. His previous boss never wanted to face the issue. Sound familiar?"

"Unfortunately, yes."

"Let's say you can't make Jack a specialist because he doesn't have the skills anymore to be a specialist. So, what do you do?"

"I don't know," I said.

"What many people do is distort the organizational structure to accommodate Jack. They create a new group for him, something that won't get in the way. That is called structuring around an individual need. What did we say earlier? An individual cannot succeed at the expense of the organization, because then the organization suffers. That is what would happen if you create a group for Jack. Jack's function isn't needed and Jack is not an effective manager."

"So, what do you do? Throw him out on the street?"

"There is no easy answer as to what to do, but you must not sacrifice the organizational good for the individual. It's difficult, I know, but you must be very careful about the compromises you make in the organizational structure in order to accommodate an individual. The real lesson here is that a situation like this should never progress this far. It is terribly unfair to Jack and to the organization. We'll talk more about this when we talk about managerial relationships."

"I can hardly wait."

**Organizational Structure Principle No. 4: An
organization, in theory at least, should be
constructed to accommodate any and all work
without making changes in the structure.**

"I guess you don't want to be reorganizing all the time," I said.

"That's right. As long as the organizational mission remains the
same, the organizational structure should be semi-permanent. You do
not want to be changing the structure every time a new piece of work
enters the organization. If the structure is based on functions, the
structure should be relatively constant because functions are relatively
constant. Activities within functions are also relatively constant
although the way they are grouped together might change. The ways
activities are performed do change, and change frequently, but changing the way you do something doesn't usually require a change in the
organizational structure. Remember the law firm example? There
will always be a need for an accounting function and probably for
many of the activities within accounting such as accounts receivable
and general ledger. The way those activities are done will change frequently. The activities and functions themselves should change infre-
quently."

"Aren't you limiting the flexibility of an organization?"

"No. In fact, I think a properly structured organization, set up to
accommodate a variety of types and volume of work, is *more* flexible.
Flexibility doesn't mean constant structural change; it means adjust-
ment and accommodation. As the goals of the organization change or

as significant changes in the business occur, the organization may need to change its structure. That's good. It should be reevaluated regularly to see if the structure is serving the organization as well as it might. But, if you have to restructure every time a new piece of work comes into the organization, I would call that chaos, not flexibility."

"I guess you're right."

> **Organizational Structure Principle No. 5**: A span of control for a manager should be limited to the number of activities that an individual can effectively manage.

"I assume by span of control you mean the number of subordinates that a manager has," I said.

"That's the traditional definition. I would expand the definition to also include activities that must be managed."

"But I thought there was some magic number of subordinates that constituted an optimum span of control?" I asked.

"A span of control is not composed of magic numbers. There is no magic number of subordinates. There is no magic number of activities. The optimum span of control will depend on the scope of the activities to be managed, the complexity of the work, the type of function, the goals of the function, etc. A span of control of three people might be the maximum in one situation, while a span of control of twenty might be the maximum in another situation. Whatever allows a manager to effectively manage."

"How would you define effectively manage?"

"That's what we're spending three days discussing."
"Of course. What a silly question."

"And, when a manager learns to manage effectively, his span of control can generally be increased which translates into a flatter organization. But, in order to flatten an organization *effectively*, managers must do what they are supposed to do - *manage*."

"We'd better break for lunch," she said. "I need some energy for the coming battle."

'Battle?' I thought. "What battle is that?" I asked.

"The battle over accountability, everyone's favorite subject."

I couldn't see why we should battle over accountability. Accountability was simple.

"Before we break, let me outline what we've covered so far," she said.

THE ORGANIZATION:

*common goal
*specialization
*interdependence
*formal entity & under direction

*individual must not succeed at expense
 of the organization
*only as strong as weakest unit
*decisions made at lowest level possible

Organizational Structure:

*map of resources
*reporting relationships
*organize to fulfill common goal
*span of control = what can be
 effectively managed

ROLES IN AN ORGANIZATION:

SPECIALISTS:

*do the work

MANAGERS:

* direct the work

Lunch

(George Kenning)

After we ordered lunch, the consultant asked me to tell her about how I had come to hear of the Kenning Principles. I told her about the events of the past few weeks: about the meeting with my boss and the President of Sea Life and about my subsequent search for the fundamentals of management. Then, I asked her why the Kenning Philosophy wasn't very well-known in the U.S.

"Well, there's never been a book available in the U.S. about his management philosophy, so the only people who know about it are those who came into contact with George Kenning personally. That certainly limited his exposure. Also, George Kenning only spent about half of each year consulting in the U.S. The rest of the time he spent in Norway."

"What was he doing in Norway?" I asked.
"Consulting with Norwegian companies about management."

"How did he end up there?"
"George became a consultant in the mid-fifties. At that time, the

Norwegian government wanted someone to determine what kinds of managerial problems Norwegian industry would be facing in the coming years. George Kenning was chosen as their consultant. After he completed his governmental project, the companies he had observed and assessed invited him to come back and consult with them on management. He went back for about six months out of every year. In fact, he was knighted by the King of Norway in 1978 for his contributions to Norwegian industry. Then a Norwegian book that was written about his Principles became a best seller. He's quite well known over there."

"So George wasn't an academic then?"

"Definitely not. He developed the Principles based on personal observation and experience. He had some formal training in management, an MBA, but he didn't think much of it. He was trained in philosophy, and I think that is what taught him to look under the surface of things and ask the basic questions. He spent almost 30 years looking for the fundamentals before he formalized his Philosophy of Management."

"What kind of real world experience did he have?" I asked.

"He worked for General Motors for 20 years."

"What he do at GM?"

"He started on the shop floor as a tool maker, a specialist. His experience as a specialist shaped a lot of his thinking about management. Then, because of his strong feelings about the rights of workers, he became a union organizer. That was in the 30's. In 1940, he switched sides and went into management, where he stayed for fourteen years. His last assignment at GM was in Antwerp, Belgium, as Director of Administration. Antwerp had been GM's largest overseas plant until it was destroyed during World War II. George went to Belgium to help reconstruct the plant. He didn't know the language and he had never worked in personnel.   There was no building and no workers.   George's accomplishments in Antwerp included hiring 3,500 people in 3 years and successfully negotiating with the union so that, in spite of the fact that other automotive plants were closed down with frequent strikes, the GM plant never lost a single day of operations.

"What I think that assignment confirmed for George was that management did not depend on job know-how; management was a profession unto itself. After four years in Belgium, George decided to do what he had wanted to do for a long time: become a consultant."

Other, more mundane topics consumed the rest of our discussion over lunch. Then it was time to get back to work.

Accountability

6

"What is accountability?" she asked.

"It's being held accountable for what happens. No, that's defining something by itself. It's being held responsible for what happens, for the decisions you make." I remember smiling to myself, thinking how smart I was. I came to realize later how little I had understood about accountability.

"That's a common definition of accountability. The Kenning Principles use a slightly different definition." She got up to write and I dutifully copied down what she wrote in my notebook.

> **Accountability is the recognition and acceptance that one is answerable for whatever happens within an area of activity, regardless of cause. Accountability is exclusive to the management function.**

I considered the definition. I agreed with it until I got to the end of the first sentence, "What does 'regardless of cause' mean? Does it mean that no matter what happens in my area, on my ship, I'm accountable?"

"That's exactly what it means. Accountability is not concerned with cause or blame or who did what to whom. Accountability means you are given an area, a part of the common goal, to take care of. You are to make something happen within your area, and then you must answer for what did or did not happen.

"Remember XYZ? We divided the common goal into functions," she said as she drew.

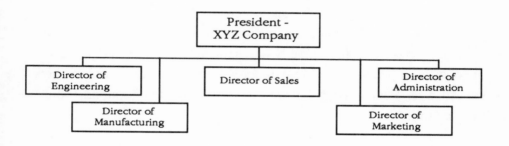

"Each function is an area of activity or an area of accountability. One manager is assigned to direct each area. That manager must answer for what happens in that area. In the sales area, for example, the sales director is accountable for making sure the sales function is helping the organization reach its goal. The sales director is accountable for everything that happens in sales, including meeting a global sales budget. By meeting the budget, he fulfills his accountability."

"That's common sense," I said, "but the problem arises when the sales director has to depend on others outside his area, and they don't do what they're supposed to do. For example, what if manufacturing makes a defective product, causing the sales director to fall short of his budget? Is the sales director accountable for that?"

"He is accountable for meeting his budget."

"But it was manufacturing's fault."

"We defined accountability as excluding fault. If we are looking for whose accountability it was to meet the global sales budget, we simply find out whose area global sales is. In this case, it's the sales director's area, so he's accountable. It's very simple."

"Don't you care whose fault it is? How are you going to make sure it doesn't happen again?"

"Finding out what went wrong and who was at fault might be useful learning tools for preventing recurrences in the future, but they're not a part of assigning accountability."

Then she asked, "Who do *you* think is accountable for the sales budget?"

"Well, the sales director is accountable, but he didn't fail in his accountability because of the circumstances. Manufacturing messed up," I said.

"What if sales had insisted on manufacturing making the product in half of the time needed to produce a quality product? What if manufacturing had warned sales what would happen, and sales had said to go ahead anyway?"

"Well, that would change everything. Then sales would have failed. It would have been their fault."

"And what if there was new competition in the market that was not addressed in the marketing campaign, and that also contributed to lost sales. Would the sales director have fulfilled his accountability then?"

"I think it's getting confusing."

"Of course it's confusing. The reason it's confusing is because everyone depends on everyone else. That's a given. So, instead of trying to untangle the maze of what happened and why, we define accountability as something that doesn't depend on circumstances and fault and who did what to whom. We know ahead of time what everyone is accountable for, and we know immediately if someone fulfilled his accountability or not.

"If you define accountability as the Kenning Principles have done, you know who is accountable regardless of circumstances. You know who is accountable *before* something goes wrong. That allows you to focus more on prevention than finger-pointing. Accountability in the Kenning system is constant. Everyone knows what they're accountable for and what everyone else is accountable for. You don't wait until things go wrong to worry about accountability. You determine it up front and then things have a better chance of not going wrong in the first place."

"I can see value in that. Sometimes people spend more time trying to figure out whose fault something was than just fixing it and then figuring out how to avoid the mistake in the future."

"Exactly. Assigning accountability regardless of cause avoids a common principle of management called the witch hunt principle of management. Witch hunt principle no. 1: When something goes wrong, find the dirty b_____ whose fault it was and hang him. What happens when that principle is used? People spend most of their time covering their tracks. They spend their time being defensive instead of making something happen. Under the Kenning Principles, there's no paper to hide under. If it's your area, you're accountable."

"What about acts of God? What if lightning strikes and knocks out the manufacturing equipment and I'm the manager of manufacturing? Am I accountable?"

"You're accountable to produce what you committed to produce.

You're accountable for meeting your goal. The cause of the failure to meet the goal doesn't matter in terms of deciding accountability."

"How can someone be accountable for an act of God?"

"You're not. You're accountable to produce what you committed to produce. If lightning can cause you problems, maybe you should invest in lightning rods or back-up generators. You're managing that area, so you are expected to worry about those factors that might impact on your ability to fulfill your accountability." She sat back and looked at me, as if she was waiting for my next objection.

Not to disappoint her, I proceeded, "Let me try another example. Let's say I'm the manager of manufacturing and my boss, the president, makes a decision without consulting me that affects my area of accountability. Doesn't my boss then assume the accountability for the outcome of that decision?"

"No. Anything that happens in your area is your accountability. Accountability and decision-making are not the same thing. A manager has to account for the results of other people's decisions, such as decisions made by subordinates, by a boss, or even those made by peers."

"What if the boss makes a mistake? Then the subordinate is the fall guy."

"The boss and the subordinate depend on each other. The boss isn't going to make decisions with the intent of letting his subordinate fail. That would be insanity. The subordinate has a piece of the boss's accountability to fulfill."

"I don't follow you."

"The president of XYZ Company, for example, has the whole company as her area of accountability. This area is too large for one person to handle, so she gets some help. She divides up her area into five functions, and she assigns a manager to take care of each function. They each have been given a piece of her accountability."

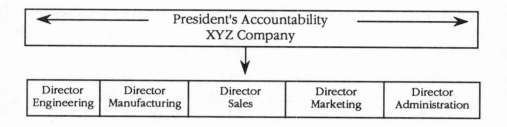

"The president is not going to do anything to deliberately allow her managers to fail because then she would also be failing in a piece of her accountability. The same holds true as you divide up accountability into smaller and smaller chunks. The regional sales manager is depending on his district sales managers to fulfill their accountabilities - that's the only way the regional manager can fulfill his accountability. So why would a sane boss allow his subordinates to fail?"

"Yes, but it doesn't sound like the real world."

"Maybe not, but how else should the real world operate? The bottom line is that you can't have an interdependent system and not depend on others. Since you must depend on others, then it's in your best interest to make sure they're successful."

"So a manager is accountable for everything that happens in his area," I said incredulously.

"Yes. If something goes wrong, we ask, 'Whose area is it? Who was supposed to be taking care of that piece?'"

"You seem to focus on failure a lot," I complained.

"That's not my intent. Accountability involves both success and failure. Most people don't have a problem accepting accountability for success, even if some of the factors that contributed to that success were beyond their control, or not their doing, or not their decision. If managers can accept the concept of accountability when they are successful, they must also accept it when they are not. A manager must accept that everything that happens in his area is his. His job is to take care of an area and the resources entrusted to him in that area. A manager simply doesn't have control over everything that he must account for. The irony is that the only way to get true control is to give it up."

"I was following you until that last remark."

"Accountability always brings up the issue of control. Control and accountability are not the same thing. When a manager is given accountability for everything that happens in an area, a natural response is to try to control everything in that area, but that's impossible to do. That's why the manager was given help in the form of resources in the first place - because the area was too big for one person to handle alone. The manager cannot control everything, so he must let go. He must develop those under him to take care of their piece of the whole. Only by learning to let go and depend on others does the manager end up with *real* control over outcomes - it's indirect, but it's much more powerful and much more productive."

I hadn't thought much about the issue of accountability before. I always felt accountable as a manager for things inside my area, inside of my control. I began to think about the overwhelming nature of accountability as it was being described to me and the inclination to try to do everything oneself in order not to fail. I could also see that one had to let go, but I also knew how difficult that was.

"Depending on others is not easy," she said as if reading my mind. "Some people are better at it than others. But, it's something that comes with the manager's role. It's part of interdependence."

"It all seems so overwhelming. How can you fulfill this accountability if you can't control what happens?"

"You're not powerless as a manager. Fulfilling accountability will be the subject of much of our discussions over the next two days. First, we need to make sure the concept is clear, then we'll move on to fulfillment."

"What about the specialist? Isn't he accountable?"

"No, the manager accounts for the tasks the specialist does. The specialist is only expected to do those things that are assigned to him, with the resources provided. If he fails, his manager must account for that failure. The specialist is not accountable. He's responsible."

"But, what's the difference? I thought they were synonyms?"

Responsibility 7

"Even though accountability and responsibility are listed as synonyms in the dictionary," she said, "the Kenning Principles clearly differentiate between the two terms. We already defined accountability. Here is the Kenning definition of responsibility."

> **Responsibility is the fulfillment of specified tasks or assignments and satisfaction of job obligations as delegated by a manager (boss) to a specialist (subordinate).**

"How is delegation defined?" I asked.

Delegation is the creation of an opportunity for a specialist to be of assistance in the fulfillment of a manager's accountability. A manager delegates responsibility to a specialist, but retains accountability.

"So, you're saying that a manager is accountable and a specialist is responsible."

"Right."

"And, delegation is to assign tasks or assignments to a specialist. In other words, to assign responsibility."

"Right again. The specialist takes direction from the boss. The specialist must do the assignments or tasks as assigned by the boss. The specialist must also satisfy the obligations of the job, such as working so many hours a day. Those are his responsibilities. The manager must account for the results of the specialist's tasks. He must account for how the resources entrusted to him were used. Responsibility is doing what I have been directed to do. Accountability is answering for what happens."

"So, if I am a specialist, and I don't do my work assignment properly, then it's my boss who has to answer for that?"

"That's right. Your boss is accountable for the results of your work. If your task was not done properly, he probably didn't provide you with the proper training, or he must not have given you the proper direction, or the proper resources. Maybe he picked the wrong person to do the job in the first place. It's the manager's job to get something done through others, and he's the one who has to answer for what happens."

"So, if the specialist does something wrong, a manager can't tell his boss he failed in his accountability because of an error by a specialist."

"That's right. It was the manager's accountability. The manager failed, not the specialist. Besides, we don't care what the reasons for the failure were, because accountability is without cause or blame."

"It seems like the specialist gets off easy."

"Maybe. But, he has a different job to perform than the manager. People have to decide which role they are best suited to. Both roles are equally important to the organization. If someone's strength lies in doing the work, he might be best suited to being a specialist. If someone's strength lies in directing others and accounting for the outcome, then he might be better suited to be a manager. The organization needs good specialists just as it needs good managers, but they are two different jobs. If you're a manager you get accountability; if you're a specialist, you don't."

"Being a manager, under your definition, seems like a difficult task."

"It is. Accountability is a hard concept to accept, but in order to be a manager, you must accept accountability."

"You're pretty tough."

"You'd better be tough, too. We aren't talking about fantasy land here. We're talking about trying to keep the ship afloat and speeding towards its destination. Your organization can't afford the luxury of having mini-empires with all their own resources because they're afraid to depend on anyone for anything. You don't have time for finding fault. You've got to run an efficient operation in order to go someplace quickly. Otherwise, your ship might sink. You need to divide up the work burden and put someone who understands accountability in charge of each piece, someone who understands that his role is to make things happen through others. Those are the kind of managers you need, because that's what management is all about."

We took a short break, and I mulled over what she had just covered. I couldn't quite accept that a manager could be accountable for everything and the specialist not accountable at all. The consultant said this was how most people reacted. She still hadn't convinced me, but she said not to worry. We weren't done with accountability yet.

Accountability Revisited

8

"I'm still not convinced that your defintion of accountability makes sense," I said. "If the president of XYZ Company is accountable for everything that happens in the company, doesn't that mean that she's also accountable if one of the district sales managers doesn't fulfill his accountability to meet a budget goal?"

"Why do you think that?" she asked.

"If the district manager doesn't meet his budget goal, that will have an impact on the organization, so, somehow, the president has to have a piece of that failure."

"Maybe it would help if we looked at the division of accountability a little differently." She drew a new picture of the XYZ Company.

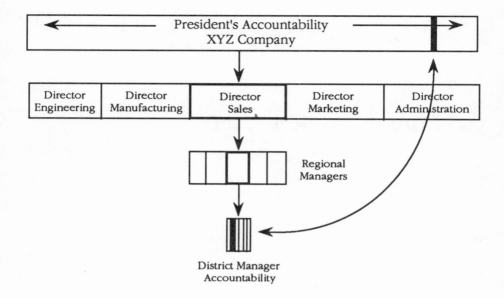

"The darkened area," she said, "is the area of accountability of one district manager. Even if you assume he failed in all of his accountability, as represented by the blackened rectangle, that still represents a miniscule slice of the president's accountability. Accountability works like decision making: you want to push it down to the lowest possible level, excluding the specialist, of course. So, if the district sales manager does not meet his budget, that's his accountability. If he continues to fail in his accountability, we are going to look at his boss, the regional sales manager, and ask, 'Why are you letting your subordinate fail?' If the regional sales manager repeatedly fails, then we will look to the sales director and so on. Eventually we might look to the president, but we would look to her because one or more of her managers failed, not because a district sales manager failed. The president's job is to worry about making her direct subordinates, the directors, successful."

"That seems clear."

"Having said that, there are instances where a success or failure of a lower level manager might impact the accountability of the president. An example would be the *Exxon Valdez* accident. Since the failure of a lower level manager significantly affected the entire company, at least in my view, all levels of management above the *Valdez* captain also failed in their accountabilities. Of course, this is an extreme case."

"And one too close to home. But, I'm still uncomfortable with all this talk about failure."

"Too many managers equate failure with getting a demotion or getting fired. I wonder about the healthiness of an organization where the threat of failure is so enormous. Failure does not necessarily mean you're going to get fired. The consequence of a failure depends on the nature of the failure and the extent to which the failure impacts the organization. The repercussion of failing might be as simple as your boss saying, 'You failed,' or if the impact were large, he might say, 'You won't receive a raise this year.' He might even say, 'You're fired,' but that's rare. If you succeed, he's not necessarily going to say, 'You get a promotion,' either. There is no magic formula for what the consequences will be of fulfilling or not fulfilling accountability. It depends on the situation.

"The managers I envision accept that even though they want to succeed, they are going to fail now and then. They accept that making something happen often involves letting other people make some mistakes in order to learn and grow, and they accept that the manager is accountable for the mistakes of his subordinates."

"You've been talking about being accountable for both an area and goals. How do they differ?"

"You are accountable for everything that happens within your area and you are accountable for the specific goals within that area. If someone gets hurt in your area, you're accountable, even if it didn't impact on one of your goals. Goals are set to help the area accomplish something specific. For example, let's assume you're accountable for a manufacturing plant. You must answer for everything that goes on in that plant. You must also answer for the goals of the plant, such as making X number of widgets each year within certain quality and cost requirements referred to as Y. If you are given goals that you can't accept, you're going to have to negotiate them."

"This is the first I've heard of negotiating anything."

"Your area of accountability is generally not very negotiable. Your boss assigns you an area to manage. The area is generally defined by him, because it's a position that he has established. It's part of the structure of the organization. The area can be described by a position description. For example, it might be sales region one which includes the following states... Within that area there are goals or performance standards that support the organizational goal. There might be short-term and long-term goals. Those goals are negotiable.

Area of accountability = Assigned by boss
Goals and objectives = Negotiated with boss

"You must accept the accountability to fulfill the goals in your area, but if the goals being proposed are not ones you think you can fulfill, then you'd better get them changed. You are not a powerless receiver of orders from above. You are a manager, and you know your area and what it can do better than anyone else. You had better fight to get the appropriate goals set for your area, because in the end you are going to be held accountable for them."

"So, just because my boss tells me he wants me to do something, doesn't mean I have to do it?"

"That's right. If you can't fulfill the accountability he is assigning you, then you'd better get him to change his mind."

"So I determine what accountability I'll accept within my area?"

"In terms of goals, yes. Your boss, however, does have the final say. He can put his foot down and say, 'You will do such and such.' Either you accept that accountability or you convince him to change his mind. In the end, you must come to an agreement, and then the negotiated goals become your goals, because you have accepted the accountability for them. Keep in mind that your boss is trying to make you successful, so he's not going to give you goals that will cause you to fail. Let's move on to the Principles of Accountability."

<u>Accountability Principle No. 1</u>: Acceptance of accountability is the key factor in determining if a manager is a manager.

"You said before that if you can't accept accountability, you're not a manager."

"If a manager accepts the concept of accountability, as I have described it, then he becomes a manager in more than just title. There is an attitude that goes with managing that has to do with accepting the challenge and burden of accountability. It says that as a manger, you are making something happen through others, and then you accept the consequences, without excuses or blame."

<u>Accountability Principle No. 2</u>: An area of accountability must be defined. It might be defined by one's immediate superior, or, if not, the limits must be sought.

"It seems clear that you've got to know what are the limits of the area that you're accountable for. You said the area can be defined in a position description. So, if a position description doesn't exist, it would make sense for the boss and the subordinate to sit down and discuss what the subordinate's area of accountability is. If this doesn't happen, I guess what you're saying is that if you're a manager, there aren't any excuses for not knowing what you're accountable for. It's your option - well, you've defined it as more than an option, it's your requirement to find the boundaries of your accountability."

"Excellent. There can't be pieces of accountability that are not assigned. They've all got to be covered. If you can't get your boss to define your area of accountability, you might have to keep testing the boundaries until you're told, 'That's far enough.'"

Accountability Principle No. 3: Acceptance of accountability must be complete and without qualification.

"We discussed this earlier. The definition of accountability said that one is answerable regardless of cause which is the same thing as without qualification."

"Right again. See how easy this is? Try number four."

Accountability Principle No. 4: Accountability is not shared; neither is authority.

"Accountability not being shared seems straightforward. Everyone has a distinct area of accountability, and if it's in your area, it's yours. But, what about the situation where a service group, like a computer systems group, is accountable for maintaining the computer systems that run the manufacturing plant, and the system breaks down, causing the plant to have to shut down. Isn't the accountability for that failure shared between the computer manager and the manufacturing manager?"

"No. There are two different accountabilities. The computer systems group is accountable for the effective operation of all computer systems. If a computer system fails, then the computer manager failed. The manufacturing manager also failed, not because the computer system didn't work, but because he didn't produce what he committed to produce. Both managers failed, but they failed in different accountabilities."

"I see."

"What about the part that says authority is not shared?" she asked.

I struggled with that concept, "For one area there is only one authority?"

"Good. This concept means we have one person who gives direction for a certain area. We have one person who is the manager for the area, and he is the only authority for that area to his subordinates. He is the boss to the subordinates in that area."

Accountability Principle No. 5: Fulfillment of accountability is the basis upon which a manager's performance is evaluated.

"If you didn't evaluate a manager's performance based on the fulfillment of accountability, it would be meaningless," I said.

"You're right. Without consequence, accountability or anything else, for that matter, is meaningless. Any questions on accountability?"

"I'm still not clear on negotiating goals."

"The setting of goals is interactive. Your boss sets direction. Maybe you come up with the goals; maybe he does. You and your boss discuss the proposed goals. You might argue about the goals. Maybe you get help from other managers to argue your position. In the end, you come to an agreement. Then the goals are your goals; they are your performance standards. You accept accountability for fulfilling the standards."

"What you're presenting makes me see the boss and subordinate not in a top down relationship, but in an interactive, dynamic relationship where both are trying to realize the organization's objectives together."

"I think you've got it. To me, the true value of accountability is that it allows an organization to operate as a team and at the same time preserve the strength of the individual. It forces a manager to do what he is supposed to do which is to get things done through others. It forces him to train subordinates. It forces him to ensure that others in the organization are successful.

"Let's review the flow chart of what we've covered so far, and then we'll break for the day. Tomorrow we'll move on to organizational accountability."

"What, *more* accountability?"

THE ORGANIZATION:

* common goal
* specialization
* interdependence
* formal entity & under direction

* individual must not succeed at expense of the organization
* only as strong as weakest unit
* decisions made at lowest level possible

Organizational Structure:

* map of resources
* reporting relationships
* organize to fulfill common goal
* span of control = what can be effectively managed

ROLES IN AN ORGANIZATION:

SPECIALISTS:

* do the work

MANAGERS:

* direct the work

Responsibility:

* do tasks & assignments
* fulfill job obligations

Accountability:

* answer for results of others
* everything within area
* goals & objectives
* regardless of cause

Day Two

Organizational Accountability 9

We started our session at 8 a.m. sharp.

"Yesterday," she said, "we talked about accountability. Do you have any remaining questions?"

"Not at the moment," I responded.

"Good. The accountability we discussed yesterday is called functional accountability. That would be the accountability you have for your ship. You have another accountability to consider: organizational accountability. Your ship is part of a larger organization: Global Enterprises. You are also accountable for Global Enterprises."

It seemed to me that just taking care of my functional accountability was going to take all my time. "What exactly is organizational accountability?"

Organizational accountability is the accountability to be of practical assistance in the realization of any organizational objectives. It is required of all managers.

"Let me explain," she said. "As we discussed before, everyone in an organization depends on the success of the overall organization. The people who guide the organization, the managers, have an accountability to make sure the organization, as a whole, is successful. They fulfill this organizational accountability by helping to realize organizational objectives."

"What purpose does organizational accountability serve?" I asked.

"It keeps each of the units tied together and working for the common good, and it ensures that everyone acts under the principle of interdependence. Another important reason for organizational accountability is that when the organization is divided into parts, or functions, the conscience of the organization gets fragmented. It's the, 'It's not my area syndrome,' or, 'I don't need to worry about that.' Organizational accountability says every manager is the conscience for the whole. The whole, then, is also every manager's area."

"Are you saying I need to mind everyone else's business?" I asked.

"Yes and no. If someone else's business is hurting the organization, then it becomes your concern or your organizational accountability to do something. However, organizational accountability is used primarily to make sure that the resources entrusted to you as a manager are used to further organizational objectives."

"So I have a functional accountability to get something done, call it *X*, and someone else wants me to use my resources for something that's more important to the organization, call it Y. Then, does organizational accountability mean I should move my resources from X to Y?"

"Yes."

"What if that means I fail in my accountability to do X?"

"You would probably want to renegotiate your functional accountability with your boss. Maybe he will change your accountability for X. Maybe he won't. But, you know the organization needs Y. You need to figure out some way to make Y happen. Organizational accountability requires that managers try to satisfy the most important organizational needs with the resources available."

"What are the consequences of fulfilling or not fulfilling your organizational accountability?" I asked.

"Evaluating the fulfillment of organizational accountability is not as clear cut as evaluating functional accountability, since there will not be universal agreement about what's best for the organization, but it should still be part of the performance evaluation of a manager. The acceptance of organizational accountability is reflected in an attitude, that of putting the common organizational goals ahead of individual goals."

"Can you give me an example of organizational accountability?"

"Suppose you receive information that one of the ships in your department might be hit by terrorist fire. Are you accountable for doing something about that?"

"Of course, I'd warn them of the attack."

"What if they didn't listen to you?"

"Then I'd go over their heads, until someone did listen to me," I stated.

"Then you would be fulfilling your organizational accountability. However, most of the time organizational accountability is not so clear cut. For example, let's suppose you discovered a way to route ships between ports using a new computer program that could save the company ten million dollars a year. Routing is not part of your functional accountability. You propose this to the proper department at Global, but they're not interested. You talk to your boss, but he tells you to drop it. 'You've tried,' he says, 'but they aren't interested in using computers to do their routing.' Have you fulfilled your organizational accountability?"

"It sounds like I did. You can't make someone do what they don't want to do."

"Yes, but the organization will lose ten million dollars a year if it doesn't use your idea. That's a waste of money, and, as a manager, you're a trustee for the organization. How can you allow this money to be wasted? Organizational accountability requires that you take care of the organization, making sure that it is healthy and strong. So, you can't forget it. You'll have to keep trying. Otherwise, you'll fail in your organizational accountability."

"Even if the department doesn't want it?"

"Maybe you haven't explained it to them properly. How could they not want to save ten million dollars a year? Remember, this is your organization. Your job as a manager is to keep the organization moving forward, toward its goal. You have to worry about the whole. That's part of your job. Otherwise, what do we end up with? A bunch of independent empires. Organizational accountability ties all the units together by requiring that everyone be on the same team."

"That makes sense," I said.

"Now that you understand accountability, we're going to move on to looking at the role of the manager in depth. We'll cover Organizational Accountability Principles tomorrow as a wrap-up."

The Role of the Manager   10

"How about taking a shot at the definition of a manager?" she asked.

"A manager is someone who provides direction, and a manager is someone who has accountability, both for a functional area and for the organization as a whole."

"That's close. How does a manager fulfill his accountabilities?"

"Through the use of resources?"

"Excellent. And, the most important resource is people. The definition then becomes:"

> **A manager is someone who is accountable for making something planned happen within a specific area through the use of available resources. Management is direction; it is neither consensus nor example.**

I said, "This definition makes it clear that managers are expected to do something, not just push papers. I like that."

"I hope managers are doing something. With the accountability they've been given, they'd better be spurred into action. And, that action should be making something happen through others."

"The second part of the definition refers to consensus," I said. "I know we discussed that decisions aren't made by consensus, and I can understand that you can't always manage by consensus, but isn't there value in using consensus to get buy-in so that decisions will be more readily accepted?"

"Although getting consensus or buy-in can be a useful management tool in certain situations, it's not a principle of management. If it were, it would say a manager must have a consensus in order to manage. That would bring the organization to a standstill. Besides, you don't have to have consensus to get buy-in. A better way to get buy-in is to utilize people's expertise before arriving at a decision. As you'll see, that is one of the management principles we'll discuss tomorrow. People's skills, talents, and knowledge should be utilized if you want to make the best possible decisions for the organization. The manager must utilize resources to get something done and part of utilizing resources is drawing out their expertise. That involves them in the decision making process without resorting to consensus."

"Okay. I can agree with that, but what's this statement about management is not by example? All the management experts talk about managing by example."

"If we take the management experts' advice, we'd have to turn the management principle around so it said: you must manage by example. Now, let's also suppose you're a first line manager. Therefore, the people you are managing are specialists. You have accountability; you provide direction. They have responsibility; they do the work.

Let's also suppose that you don't have the know-how to do the jobs of your specialists. How can you set an example?"

"You don't have to set an example in the specific tasks, but you do have to set an example in work habits."

"So, if they work 9 to 5, you must also?"

"You should work at least that long."

"Maybe 8 to 6?"

"Right."

"I'm going to give you a promotion. You manage a manufacturing facility with three shifts. How can you set an example for all three shifts? By working at the facility 24 hours a day?"

"No. The example I would set would be to work hard at least eight hours a day. The workers need to know I'm working as hard as they are."

"What if you have to go to a meeting at headquarters during the afternoon and so you have to leave early? Do you explain to your subordinates what is happening, so they'll know you are still setting a good example and they won't leave early too, trying to follow your lead?"

"You're not being reasonable with these examples. All I am saying is you should be working hard, and you shouldn't be a goof-off, if you don't want your people to goof-off."

"Oh, I can agree that we don't want goof-offs in management. Management is hard work - in fact it's a 24 hours a day job."

"Well, I wouldn't go that far. Maybe 9 or 10 hours."

"So you stop being a manager when you leave the plant?"

"Of course."

"Are you a parent?"

"Yes."

"How many hours a day are you a parent?"

"I'm always a parent."

"Right, and because of accountability, you're always a manager. If the plant blows up at midnight, you're still accountable. So, the demands of the manager's job may be such that the manager and the specialist have different work habits. The specialist's performance cannot be dependent on his manager setting a 'good' example for him. Rather it depends on his manager setting clear direction for him. In addition, we tend to forget that there is a basic contract between an individual and an organization that says you, the individual, agree to perform such and such a job assignment and in return, the organization agrees to pay you such and such remuneration.

"I'm not saying that setting an example cannot be a valuable tool at times, but managing others cannot depend on setting an example. Managers must be able to get something done by simply telling others what they want done."

"Although I guess you're right, what about the argument that setting an example is a motivational tool?"

"My approach is much more straightforward. First, set the direction for your area. Then, set fair, honest and safe performance standards for what is expected, and let people know if they are meeting the standards. If they're not, help them get back on target.

"If you follow the Principles of Management, I don't think you'll have much trouble in the motivational area. The problem with motivational techniques is that you're often trying to cure the symptom and not the disease. You need to get at the cause of the lack of motivation, and very often it's not a lack of consensus or example setting, and it's not unmotivated specialists; it's poor management."

I thought she was a bit hard on management, but I let it pass.

"Let's try some Principles," she said.

Manager Principle No. 1: Only a manager has accountability. The burden of accountability distinguishes the manager from the specialist.

"Now that I understand the full meaning of accountability, I think I understand why specialists aren't accountable. If they were, they'd have the job of the manager, as well as the job of the specialist, which would limit the time they'd have to actually do the work. That wouldn't be very productive."

"You catch on quickly."

"It seems the hardest management job is at the first line," I said.

"Why do you think that?" she asked.

"It seems to me that the interface between the manager and specialist could be a source of conflict since they have different roles in the organization. The other thing that strikes me about the difficulty at the first line is that pressure comes down from above and lands on the first line manager, because he's the one who has to see to it that the work gets done. "

"Good point. What *should* happen is that in addition to the requirements for work filtering down, support for getting the work done should also filter down. Each manager, from the top of the organization to the first line, should be helping his subordinates be successful. When this occurs, each level of mangement is focused on the level below until, essentially, the entire management team is supporting the first line. Let me show you."

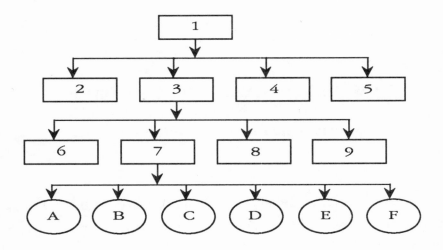

She pointed to her chart and said, "Number 1 is supporting 2, 3, 4 and 5. Number 3 is supporting 6, 7, 8 and 9. Number 7 is a first line manager. He's got No. 3 looking out for him and No. 1 looking out for No. 3. Number 7 is making sure the work gets done by specialists A through F, but he's got a lot of support from above."

"So I need to be spending more time looking down to see what I can do to help my officers, than looking up to see if my boss is happy."

"Doesn't that make more sense? Certainly supporting the boss is important, but too often we forget about the top down side of support."

Manager Principle No. 2: Each manager position should be recognized within an organizational structure and should include a specific area of accountability, authority or not, subordinates or not.

"What? You don't need authority as a manager?" I asked.

"It says you can't *rely* on authority to get things done. Not having the proper authority does not relieve you of your accountability. The manager works through others and must be able to get things done by influencing others. A manager who can only manage by direct authority is not much of a manager."

"I thought you said that a manager simply tells others what to do."

"Yes, he must be able to give directions to subordinates, but they respond to his direction not because he carries a big stick, but because he's their boss, and because he's a leader. He has the ability to take others where he wants to go. If you depend on authority alone to get things done, you won't get much done. In addition, a manager has to get his peers to do things for him. Authority won't help him much there."

"That's the first time you've mentioned leadership."

"Leading is a component of managing. The manager who is also a leader will be someone who is self-assured and able to stand alone, but he must also be part of the team."

"I have another question. How can you be a manager without subordinates?"

"We said a manager was someone who gets things done through others. Although those others may be subordinates, they can also be other managers. Managers who have accountability and don't have subordinates, fulfill their accountability by getting help from other managers who do have subordinates. Project managers in a matrix structure are an example of managers who have neither subordinates nor authority."

"Wait a minute. What's a matrix?" I asked.

"It's a type of structure used in organizations which have many projects going on simultaneously, where each project requires similar types of resources. A matrix structure is organized around functions, not projects, but each project has an accountable manager who uses the resources within the functional areas to fulfill his accountability for the project. Let's take the XYZ Company and make it into a matrix structure. We do that by adding a project management group."

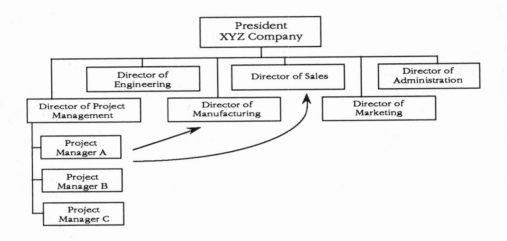

"This project management group contains an accountable manager for each product that the organization sells - although one manager could be accountable for more than one product. Let's say project manager A is accountable for widget A. Let's say she is accountable for achieving certain profitability objectives for widget A. She must work with the managers in the other functions, such as manufacturing and sales, to fulfill her accountability. Sales and manufacturing also work on widgets B and C, and must interact with project managers B and C.

"The functional managers are accountable for fulfilling their piece of each project. For example, the manufacturing manager accepts the accountability to make X number of widgets at Y quality and cost requirements. The sales manager accepts the accountability to sell Z number of widgets. The project manager's area of accountability, in this example, is widget A. She is accountable for the profitability of widget A."

"What happens if manufacturing doesn't make widget A according to the requirements, and as a result, sales go down and profitability goals are not met? Who's accountable?"

"If Project Manager A cannot meet her profitability goal, then she has failed."

"No fault accountability again."

"Right. Project Manager A failed to fulfill her accountability."

"What about the manufacturing manager ? Do he get off scot-free?"

"No. The manufacturing manager had an accountability to produce widget A according to requirements Y. He failed to do that, so he failed in his accountability. Project Manager A is not accountable for manufacturing. She is accountable for profitability. They are two separate accountabilities. Remember, you cannot share accountability."

"What is the benefit of having a matrix structure?"

"A matrix structure can accommodate a constantly changing portfolio of projects without having to change the structure. When an organization has a lot of similar projects, a matrix can be the most efficient allocation of resources. In addition, the project manager who is assigned accountability for the overall project ensures that all the pieces of the project come together; that nothing falls between the cracks. But, the success of a matrix structure depends on everyone in the organization knowing what they're accountable for."

"All I can say is that Project Manager A had better be nice to those functional managers, because she's at their mercy."

"Everyone in the organization is at everyone else's mercy, because of interdependence."

"Right. I knew that."

> **Manager Principle No. 3**: Functional accountability notwithstanding, each manager bears an organizational accountability that recognizes the essential tenet for having an organization in the first place - a common goal. A manager, therefore, must take care of peers as well as his or her boss and subordinates.

"I think we covered this this morning," I said, "at least the part about organizational accountability. A manager has to take care of his peers - help them fulfill their accountability, just as he has to take care of those who report to him and to whom he reports. So when another manager needs some help in order to fulfill his accountability, you have an obligation to help if that's what's best for the organization."

"Even if helping means you'll fail in your functional accountability?" she asked.

"Yes. You have to ask, 'What's best for the organization?'"

"That's *exactly* the question to ask!"

Manager Principle No. 4: **A manager's method of fulfilling accountability can vary, subject to the individual's style, but common management principles should prevail within an organization.**

"What I think this says is that underneath the differences in approach by various managers, there must be a common denominator, some rules or principles that everyone follows."

"That's right. Your style of managing will depend on your personality, your past experiences, your education and the culture of the organization for which you work. There is no one right style. But, there should be a set of principles that provide a guideline of what you do as a manager. The Kenning Principles are one example of a set of principles, and, of course, I think they're the best example. No matter which set of principles you choose, it's important that every manager in the organization has a common understanding of what is expected, so that everyone is operating under the same rules and marching in the same direction.

"Let's take a short break and then continue with more Manager Principles."

The Role of the Manager - **11**
Part 2

"The concept of getting things done through others is starting to take on a new meaning for me. Although I'd always considered myself a hands-off manager, I can see I have some work to do in that area."

"That enlightenment should help you explain the next Principle."

> **Manager Principle No. 5: A manager's effectiveness is not determined by job know-how or education. Management, a profession unto itself, requires enduring and cohesive drill in the management process by all managers, at all levels.**

"What do you mean by 'job know-how?'"

"The know-how to do a specialist's job."

"So, you're saying the manager doesn't need to know anything about the jobs he manages? How can you manage something you don't know anything about?"

"What this Principle says is that the manager's effectiveness is not *determined* by job know-how or education. If the manager's role is to work through others, why should it matter how much job know-how he has?"

"How can a manager provide direction if he doesn't know the job?"

"Setting direction and knowing how to do the jobs of the specialist are not the same thing. Setting direction requires looking at the big picture. Job know-how requires looking at the individual details. If we take your reasoning to its logical conclusion, someone could not manage an area unless he knew how to do each of the jobs in that area. Do you know how to do each of the jobs on your ship?"

"Well, no, but that's not exactly what I meant. For example, I couldn't have my deck officer managing the engineers. He wouldn't know what to tell them to do."

"If your deck officer manages according to the Principles, then he knows that it's not his job to swab the decks. He utilizes specialists to do that. If he has learned to manage, I contend that he could probably manage the engineers, because he would know it's not his job to run the engines, but to keep the engines running through the use of the engineers. He would have learned to utilize others to get the job done.

"A manager is an orchestra leader. He doesn't need to be able to sit and play the oboe and the violin and the french horn, etc. He is there to direct, to control, to develop, to utilize the performing resources that are available. He must get others to play to their potential.

"It's a common mistake to assume that the best specialist would also make the best manager," she said, "In fact, the skills required to manage and the skills required to be a specialist are not the same. A manager needs to utilize others to get things done, a specialist needs to do things himself. A manager needs to direct. A specialist needs to follow. A manager must worry about the group. The specialist must worry about his job assignment.

"If having job-know how and education were required for each of the jobs you managed, there would be extreme limitations on what someone could manage. How would you ever promote someone past the first line of management if he needed to be an expert in the areas he was required to manage?"

"Well, the first line of management is different. For example, I don't see how I could have managed a group of engineers, as I did early in my career, if I hadn't been an engineer myself."

"That's the usual argument, 'the first line is different.' You probably think that at that level you have to be an expert in order to have the respect of your people."

"Yes. I do."

"Well, I disagree. If there is an expectation that the manager is the expert, that expectation is created by the manager himself, because *he* thinks he needs to be the expert or 'super specialist.' He thinks he always has to have the answers to his specialists' questions. If he understood his role as a manager, he wouldn't try to be the expert. He would let his people assume that role.

"It is generally true that the manager who best utilizes resources is not the one with the most job know-how. The manager with the job know-how usually succumbs to the temptation to put his hands into the dishwater and help wash the dishes. The more the manager helps do the work, the less his people learn to do the work, and the less challenged they are to do their best."

"How can a manager who doesn't know anything about an area select the right talent? He wouldn't even know what questions to ask."

"The manager would find people with the appropriate expertise to help him select a candidate. It happens all the time. Let's say you manage an engineering group within R&D, and you need to hire someone in the biotechnology area, an area that you and your group don't know much about. What do you do?"

"Get help."

"Exactly. Essentially that's what managing is about: utilizing help. I think that if managers stopped trying to be specialists and started being managers, they'd be surprised at the results they'd achieve."

I told her I needed to take a break in order to think about this Principle for a few minutes.

She said, "Please, by all means, do some thinking. I'll be back in a minute."

I could see that a manager's job consisted of utilizing resources and if he did that effectively, he probably didn't need to know a lot about the details of what he was managing. I thought back on that first line manager's job I'd once had. My boss knew nothing about engineering, so he had no choice but to depend on me. I had thrived under his leadership. I had felt I was needed. I had felt I made a contribution to the organization. My boss got promoted and my new boss turned out to be a former engineer. Suddenly, I could do nothing right. Things had to be done his way or not at all. Eventually, I left that company. I guess I had become demoralized. I had gotten tired of being second-guessed all the time.

Maybe job know-how is not that important. Maybe putting your hands in the dishwater is counter-productive. What did seem important to me was understanding the big picture and then setting the course.

"Well?" she asked when she returned. "Where do we stand?"

"I hate to admit it, but I think you're right."

"Didn't I say you were smart? Next Principle."

Manager Principle No. 6: Managers can be moved from one function to another. A manager must have the ability to take over a number of diverse activities.

"This follows from what we just finished discussing," I said. "So, I guess I agree with this statement. If a manager cannot be moved to another function, then chances are he hasn't learned how to manage."

"That's right."

"What about providing direction?" I asked. "Isn't that a problem if you move to a new function?"

"Yes, it can be a problem for awhile, but assuming that the manager being moved is no dummy, it won't take him long to catch on. Also, I have to assume that if you decide to move a manager to a new function, you're going to make sure he has a boss and subordinates who do know the function, who can help him out while he's learning."

"Even though I agree that managers should have the ability to take over other functions," I said, "I think it hurts the organization when you move managers around. It takes time for them to get up to speed and mistakes can be made while they're learning."

"I believe," she said, "the benefits will far outweigh the risks, if a move is well thought out. That means the people chosen for the move must know how to manage, and that the subordinates and the boss of the manager being moved must be prepared to guide him for a year or so.

"Some of the benefits of such a move include the development of the subordinates. They become more effective because their new boss has no choice but to depend on them. Another benefit of moving a manager is the person who is moved usually becomes a better manager himself, because he has no choice but to manage. He doesn't have the job know-how that can get in the way of his managing.

"Besides, the risk to the organization is minimized because the manager goes into his new assignment knowing some very important things. He knows the organization. He knows how to get things done through others. He knows where to get help. In the mid- and long-term the organization will benefit from the move, if it's done properly."

"Why not just bring someone in from the outside who already knows the area?" I asked.

"For a number of reasons. First, the organization knows the strengths and weaknesses of internal candidates. Outside candidates are unknowns, so the organization takes more of a risk with them. There is no way you can know someone from the outside as well as you know your own managers. Secondly, when you bring someone from the outside into a manager's position, there are many things he has to learn before he can be effective. He must get to know the people in the organization and where to go to get things done. He must learn the policies and procedures of the organization, and he must adjust to its culture. It takes at least as long for someone from the outside to learn these components of the manager's job, as it does to teach an internal, proven manager to learn a new area.

"The final benefit to making moves internally is that it tells the management team that the organization is serious about management development. It shows a commitment to management."

"I take it you feel strongly about this."

"I do. But, don't get me wrong. I'm not saying that there aren't times when an organization might have to go outside. For example, maybe the organization is expanding so fast it can't develop enough internal candidates. However, going outside should always be a last resort. George Kenning used to say that when the president leaves, the floor sweeper should get promoted. In other words, promotion from within creates opportunity all the way down the line. When you promote one of the subordinates to president, a slot in the next line opens up. When you promote someone into that slot, another slot opens up and so on. It's the domino effect.

"Promotion from within also says you'd better be developing your subordinates to take over for you. Otherwise, you've failed as a manager. Ready to move on?"

"Yes."

Manager Principle No. 7: A manager must preserve detached and nonpersonal relationships throughout the organization.

"Does this mean I can't socialize with my fellow officers?"

"Maybe. You are in the position, as a manager, to evaluate other people's performances. To do that effectively, you must be objective, and you must *appear* to be objective. Maybe you and your first mate are good friends. You do things together socially, and so you are extra careful not to show any bias towards him. How does your friendship appear to your other officers? Do they feel you're objective? Are you *really* objective? Can you be?

"Unfortunately, being a manager carries a heavy burden. Other people's careers are in your hands, so you must be very careful in your relationships - at work and outside of work. You must judge each situation by asking, 'Will it compromise my ability to perform my manager's role objectively?' By the way, specialists have no such limitations."

"That job is looking better all the time. What about company functions? Are you saying there shouldn't be company Christmas parties?"

"Company functions can be beneficial as long as they are handled in a detached and nonpersonal manner by managers."

"What do you mean detached and nonpersonal?"

"I mean you retain your objectivity. You don't get personally involved with people you work with."

> **<u>Manager Principle No. 8</u>: Success as a manager depends upon the manager's ability to develop and utilize available resources. To maximize the use of others is a full-time occupation.**

"The first sentence is no problem. We've covered that already. I question whether maximizing the use of others is always a full-time job. What if you only have three people to manage? How can that be full-time?"

"Managing might not be a full-time profession if the manager's span of control is not large enough or if he isn't fully utilizing the resources entrusted to him. The remedy, however, is not to do the work of those who work for you. The remedy is either to spend more time developing and utilizing one's subordinates or to expand one's area of accountability. We don't want managers trying to wear the two hats of the specialist and the manager, although it happens all the time. If you aren't completely occupied as a manager, your first question should be, 'Am I doing all I could be doing to develop my subordinates?'"

"What if you do all that, but it ends up you still don't have a full-time job?"

"You mean in the real world?"

"Right."

"Well, there may be instances where you are forced to be a minotaur manager - part manager, part specialist. I strongly advise against it. However, if someone is in that spot, he needs to focus on developing his managerial skills while still trying to do his specialist tasks. It's a very difficult position to be in and one the Principles do not condone."

Manager Principle No. 9: The true value of a manager is determined by his or her contribution to the success of others.

I said, "I guess this sums up what management is all about - by making others successful, the manager is successful. It's like being a successful parent."

"If everyone in an organization acted on this Principle, there would be no limit to what the organization could accomplish," she said.

"Why, then, are so many managers afraid of having the people who report to them look good?"

"I think it's a lack of self-confidence and a lack of understanding of what the manager's role is all about. Or, maybe the organization is sending out signals suggesting that a manager's success is not dependent on the success of others. Just because some organizations haven't gotten it right, doesn't change the Principle."

"I thought not."

> **Manager Principle No. 10:** **An organization should make the criteria for manager selection, evaluation, development, and promotion common knowledge. The measurements should be known.**

"What are the criteria for managers?"

"Funny you should ask. We'll cover that right after lunch, but first, let's review what we've covered in the first day and half of your education."

THE ORGANIZATION:

- common goal
- specialization
- interdependence
- formal entity & under direction

- individual must not succeed at expense of the organization
- only as strong as weakest unit
- decisions made at lowest level possible

Organizational Structure:

- map of resources
- reporting relationships
- organize to fulfill common goal
- span of control = what can be effectively managed

Organizational Accountability:

- be of practical assistance in realization of organizational objectives
- required of all managers

ROLES IN AN ORGANIZATION:

SPECIALISTS:

- do the work

Responsibility:

- do tasks & assignments
- fulfill job obligations

MANAGERS:

- direct the work
- make something planned happen through others
- make subordinates successful

Role of Manager:

- management is direction
- effectiveness is not determined by job know-how
- can take over a number of diverse activities
- must preserve detached and nonpersonal relationships
- success depends on development and utilization of resources
- true value determined by contribution to success of others

Accountability:

- answer for results of others
- everything within area
- goals & objectives
- regardless of cause

Lunch
(Quality)

"What do you think about all the emphasis on quality?" I asked.
"I think it's about time."

"How do the Kenning Principles and quality fit together?"
"Quality is about how things get done. Phil Crosby, one of the quality gurus, says you must define what you mean by quality. You must set requirements that define specifically how you're going to measure quality. Juran, another quality expert, talks about establishing the needs of the customers, whether it's an internal or external customer. These requirements or needs, in the Kenning Philosophy, are just a part of defining a manager's objectives, so they are a part of defining what a manager is accountable for."

"What is an internal customer?"
"According to Juran a customer is anyone inside or outside the organization who is impacted by what you do in your area. In Kenning terms, internal customers are the groups that depend on you to fulfill their accountabilities. The areas that you depend on to fulfill your accountabilities would be your internal suppliers. It's simply a

way of describing interdependencies.

"Also, part of a quality improvement process involves defining what the requirements for each area are. These requirements would be included as part of the performance standards for the area."

"So," I said, "quality standards are just a part of performance standards?"

"Right. Although I'm not a quality consultant, it seems to me that a successful quality effort includes not only understanding what accountability really means, but also understanding the management process so that managers can fulfill the accountability they've been given.

"A quality process relies on the management process, which of course, includes accountability. It's all well and fine to launch a big quality improvement campaign, dedicate the organization to quality, demand quality, etc., but if the management team doesn't understand and apply the basic principles of management, you won't get very far in making quality happen. Quality depends on management. It depends on first defining accountability clearly, and then knowing how to fulfill that accountability. "

"Everything comes back to accountability, doesn't it?" I asked.

"You noticed that, huh? Quality defines how things get done, and accountability defines who takes care of what. Understanding and defining accountability should be a cornerstone of a quality improvement effort."

"I guess if you clearly define accountability," I said, "you ensure that things don't fall between the cracks, and you ensure that everyone knows specifically what they're accountable for in terms of quality."

"Exactly. The other part of the management process that is key to quality is the concept of staff relationships. Many of the quality problems arise at the interfaces between areas. We're going to talk about staff relationships this afternoon. Staff relationships are what make the concept of internal customers and suppliers work. Unless you understand how to work between groups, a quality improvement process will just end up generating a lot more committees and a lot more infighting over who is supposed to do what."

"Are you saying quality is just another how-to?"

"Not exactly. Quality is one way to describe a product or process. Cost would be another way. Quality is something a manager must manage. It is not exactly a how-to of management."

After a rather hurried sandwich, we started right in on the next subject.

Criteria for Managers

12

"What do you think the criteria for managers should be?" she asked.

"Well, a manager must be able to direct others. He must be a people person: good listener, good communicator. He needs to be good at organizing and..."

"Stop! Although those may be important skills, I'm interested in the more fundamental characteristics of the manager, those traits that enable him to fulfill the role we discussed this morning."

"Okay. Let me think. I guess he'd better be able to accept interdependence and accountability. We've certainly talked about them enough."

"Much better. Let's break down this exercise into general categories and then into specific criteria within those categories. I'll explain the categories; you explain the criteria."

"That sounds fair enough."

She drew two columns on the flip chart labeling one 'categories' and the other 'criteria.' On the left she wrote down the first category.

A. Wants and likes position

"Managing is hard work," she said. "It's a 24 hour a day job. So, if you're going to be a manager, you'd better want to be a manager, and you'd better like working through others rather than doing the work yourself. Right?"

"Right."

"Now it's your turn." Under the criteria column she wrote:

1. Accepts accountability

"One of the earlier Principles said that in order to be a manager in more than just a title, you must accept accountability, or something to that effect. So, that would have to be a criterion: someone who is willing to accept accountability."

"Right. What kind of person, do you think, can accept accountability the way we have defined it?"

"Someone who is comfortable relying on others."

"What causes them to be comfortable relying on others?" she asked.

"They're confident in themselves. They aren't afraid to fail."

"Exactly. That leads us to the next category."

B. Has strong sense of self; self-confident

She explained, "Relying on others and accepting accountability for their results requires self-confidence. I don't mean egoism. I mean knowing and feeling good about oneself. Self-confidence is a key requirement for a manager. An insecure manager cannot let go, because he feels constantly threatened by the success or failure of others, whereas managers who are self-assured can enjoy their subordinates' successes in addition to accepting their subordinates' failures."

"I agree."

1. Possesses presence

"Do you mean by 'presence' the ability to command or to lead?" I asked.

"Yes. A manager needs to stand out, since he must be able to influence others. He must be a leader, and when he directs, people must follow. A manager with presence communicates confidence, both in himself and in others."

2. Able to act and stand alone

"I thought a manager had to work through others. This seems contradictory," I said.

"For an organization to be strong, the individuals within it must be strong. Who needs automatons? You can buy robots instead. Managers need to be able to think and act on their own. They need to take the burden of the organization onto their own shoulders and do something to make it move forward. That's why they've been given accountability. Managers are the heads of their functional areas, and as such, they must be able to make decisions which, at times, will be unpopular. They must be able to stand up for what they believe.

"As we discussed earlier, management is not a system of consensus, and it's not a popularity contest. A manager must be able to act according to what he thinks is right, without worrying if everyone agrees with him or not. What do you think about that?"

"I agree," I replied. "I think a strong organization needs strong individuals."

"Exactly. You can't have a strong organization without them."

3. Does not need authority

"Well, managers have to work through others, and while it is nice if you have the proper authority, you should not need it in order to get something done. The project manager in the XYZ Company matrix example did not have authority, but she had accountability."

"Excellent."

4. Tells others what to do

"This relates to what you said about standing alone. A manager must be able to make decisions, and then communicate his decisions to others. That means he must tell others what he wants done."

"You're on a roll here," she said.

I pushed up my sleeves, ready for the next criterion.

5. Benefits from criticism

"A manager isn't always going to be right," I said. "He needs to listen to others' criticisms and correct his course accordingly. It seems self-confidence comes into play here. Someone who is confident can take criticism gracefully, evaluate the merits of the criticism, and then decide whether or not to accept it."

"I agree. Criticism is a mechanism for self-improvement, and a manager must continually strive to improve himself."

6. Admits personal deficiencies

"There's nothing worse than people who act like they think they're perfect."

"Everyone has strengths and weaknesses. When a manager can admits his deficiencies, he opens the door for others to help."

7. Learns from others

"A manager is dependent on others, so it is imperative that a manager be able to learn from others," I said.

"This learning from others is an attitude, an openness that causes others to contribute. It's remarkable how effective it is. More managers ought to try it."

8. Works with a quality of ignorance and intelligent ineffectiveness

I considered this criterion for a minute, but gave up in exasperation, "A quality of ignorance and intelligent ineffectiveness? I don't get it!"

"I must admit I love the reaction this criterion elicits in people. What it means is, if a manager seems to have the answer every time a question arises, what happens to the people around him? They become dependent on him for the answers. The need for the subordinate to work out the answer for himself disappears. But, if the manager doesn't have all the answers or doesn't seem to have the answers, which I would call a 'quality of ignorance,' then others will learn to work out the answers for themselves. If a manager has the 'quality of intelligent ineffectiveness,' others will show him how to be effective by being effective themselves. This is a positive way to develop the strengths of others."

"That makes sense, but it's a convoluted way to express a simple idea."

"Yes, but, it makes you think," she said.

"Well, that's a dirty trick," I replied.

"That summarizes the self-confidence category. Now that we've described the manager as a strong individual, let's talk about him as a member of an interde..."

"I know, an interdependent group."

"Right. The criteria we have discussed so far are key to having strong individuals in management. We also want managers who can work within an organization. We want managers who are team players."

C. Team player

She explained, "A manager must be a team player because he operates within a group. The ability to work with others is important to the manager's role."

1. Thinks and acts organizationally

This is an easy one, I thought, "A manager has organizational accountability so he has to think organizationally."
"Right."

2. Activates employee development

"Activates seems to imply that a manager must do something; he must take action to develop his subordinates. Since we said his success depends on others, he'd better develop his employees."

"Managers often think employee development means sending someone off to a training course. What it really means is allowing the subordinate to do his job, instead of the manager trying to do it for him. It means helping the employee develop his skills."

"You don't like training courses?" I asked incredulously.

"It's not a matter of liking or not liking. I'm a trainer, so I do think they have some value, but they don't substitute for one-on-one, day-to-day employee development. What often happens is that people go off to a course, and when they come back, nothing happens. There is no follow-up from the boss.

"Development of people is a manager's accountability. He may use other resources, such as training courses, to help him, but they are no substitute for one-on-one, boss-to-subordinate training and development."

3. Corrects malpractices personally

"Does this mean if a subordinate does not do what you want him to do, you must correct him personally?"

"Yes. Managers must be able to look someone in the eye and tell him what he did right and, what is usually more difficult, what he did wrong."

4. Gains satisfaction from subordinate success

"A manager gets things done through others. He doesn't do the work himself. So, he'd better get his job satisfaction from other people's success. Otherwise, he's going to be pretty miserable."

"Right. The last category deals with ethics." She added it to the list.

D. Possesses conscience or sense of internalized moral standards

"A manager must act with fairness, honesty, and a sense of what is right," she said. "In addition to the standards laid down by law and by organizational policy, he must have an internalized set of moral standards that guide his actions."

"What exactly do you mean?"

"If you remember, we said that when you divide up the whole into pieces, one of the risks is that the conscience of the whole gets lost. That is why we have organizational accountability. The manager must act as the conscience of the organization. He is a director for the organization, so he needs to act on what he thinks is right. He needs to direct the organization from an ethical point of view."

"I buy that."

"Well, that completes the Kenning list of criteria. There might be other criteria your organization will want to add, but I think these cover the basics. If you can find someone who fits this bill, you've got yourself a potential star.

"Let's take a break."

I perused the completed list of criteria.

Categories	Criteria
A. Wants and likes position	1. accepts accountability
B. Has strong sense of self; self-confident	1. possesses presence 2. able to act and stand alone 3. does not need authority 4. tells others what to do 5. benefits from citicism 6. admits personal deficiencies 7. learns from others 8. works with quality of ignorance and intelligent ineffectiveness
C. Team player	1. thinks and act organizationally 2. activates employee development 3. corrects malpractices personally 4. gains satisfaction from subordinate success
D. Possesses conscience or sense of internalized moral standards	

I thought of one or two criteria I might add, such as vision and creativity. Otherwise, the list looked fairly comprehensive to me.

Line Relationships

13

"We're going to cover the two types of relationships available to a manager within an organization. The first one is called a line relationship."

"Is that a relationship between people in a line function?" I asked.

"No, I'm not referring to how you classify functions. I'm defining a line relationship as a relationship between a boss and subordinate."

> **A line relationship is that direct, unbroken one between any individual and his or her immediate superior or his or her immediate subordinates, if any.**

She explained, "This defines the line relationship as that relationship between a boss and a subordinate. The line extends only from one subordinate to one boss and vice versa. This line should be depicted on an organizational chart as a solid line." She drew an XYZ chart again.

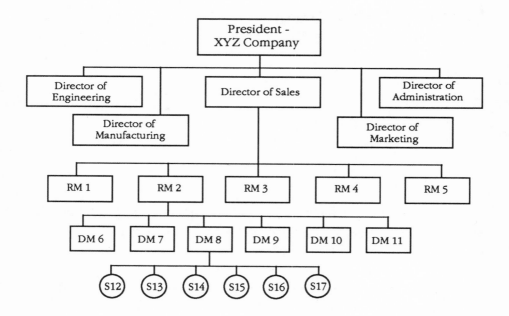

"If you recall, RM stands for regional manager, DM stands for district manager and S stands for salesperson. This chart shows that district manager 8 is the boss of salespersons 12 through 17. Regional manager 2 is the boss of district managers 6 through 11, etc. Each solid line on this chart represents a line relationship."

"I've seen some organizational charts where one person had a solid line to two people, indicating he has two bosses, I guess."

"Under the Kenning Principles you can only have one boss. That's the first Principle of the line relationship."

**Line Relationship Principle No. 1: Under all
circumstances within the structure, each person
has only one boss represented by the immediate
reporting relationship.**

"Why have a boss at all?" I asked. "There's a lot of talk about self-managed groups, so maybe you don't even need a boss."

"Frankly, I don't see it. Someone has to be the final arbitrator. Someone has to set direction. If the boss doesn't do that, who does? The group? We already talked about that when we discussed the pros and cons of consensus. Someone has to define where the group is going. Someone has to define the limits of what will or will not occur. That someone is a boss. You just can't eliminate the concept of a boss, unless you want chaos."

"What about having more than one boss. Where does that fit in with the line relationship defintion?"

"It doesn't. The concept of having two bosses is as ridiculous as not having any. When more than one person defines the direction and limits for a person or for a group of people, confusion results. What happens in a family when the parents give two different sets of rules or directions to the kids? Confusion. The same is true in a working situation. There can only be one boss and that boss sets the standards for what is expected."

"Well, couldn't you have two bosses if you were on a project temporarily? For example, another manager borrows one of my people for a project. That person then has two bosses, the project manager and myself."

"No. He only has one boss, you. Using your example, let's say you send Jeff, a specialist, to work on a project for a year. For the duration of the project, he will take work orders from the project manager, Susan. You may not see Jeff for the year, but you're still his one and only boss. You're accountable for him and for the results of his work while he's on the project. He's going to come back after the project is over, and you're going to evaluate his performance for the year he was gone, because you're his boss."

"But what if Susan doesn't give him the proper direction while he's working for her? I suppose I'm still accountable for what he does."

"You've got it. Susan has been assigned to give him work directions for the year, but Jeff is still your accountability. If Susan is causing you to fail in your accountability with Jeff, you'd better do something. I suggest you talk to Susan and try to get the situation straightened out. If that doesn't work, you might want to talk to her boss. However you decide to handle the situation, Jeff is still your accountability."

"Boy, this accountability stuff isn't easy."

"No, it's not. Let's have a go at the rest of the Principles."

<u>Line Relationship Principle No. 2</u>: The effectiveness of the line relationship is dependent on whether the individuals concerned practice what is necessary to keep it healthy.

"Having a solid line on a piece of paper doesn't mean you have a good relationship with your boss or your subordinate. It's something both parties have to work at," I said.

"Right, it's like a marriage. A good relationship means that effort is put into making the relationship work. Boss/subordinate relationships require constant attention and effort. They also require that both individuals be fair and honest, because a component of a healthy boss/subordinate relationship is a sense of mutual trust. Next Principle."

Line Relationship Principle No. 3: In a manager-to-specialist (boss/subordinate) relationship, the line relationship becomes the basis around which to delegate responsibility, to set performance standards, and to evaluate performance.

"This seems straightforward. The boss decides what needs to get done and then makes sure the expectations, or the performance standards, are clear to the specialist."

"Right."

"Isn't that easier to do with piece work than with knowledge work?" I asked.

"Yes, it probably is, but the fact that it is harder to set performance standards for knowledge work does not change the Principle that there should be standards and that the specialist should know what they are. Whoever said being a manager was easy, anyway?"

Line Relationship Principle No. 4: In a manager-to-manager (boss/subordinate) relationship, the line relationship becomes the basis around which to define and accept accountability and to recognize performance.

"This says the same thing as the last Principle, but now we're dealing with accountability instead of responsibility."

"Exactly. The boss/subordinate relationship is the most important relationship a person has in an organization. You depend on your boss and he depends on you. That doesn't mean you don't disagree, argue or fight. It means that when the dust clears, you march down the same road."

<u>Line Relationship Principle No. 5</u>: The line relationship does not limit the manager's freedom to use staff relationships.

"What is a staff relationship?"

"Funny you should ask. That's our next topic."

Staff Relationships   **14**

"I suppose a staff relationship is different than a staff position," I said.

"Right again."

> **A staff relationship is any relationship between managers which is not a line relationship. Staff relationships are used to help a manager fulfill his or her accountability; they constitute the managerial network of an organization.**

"I don't understand. You're saying that I have a staff relationship with every manager in the organization?"

"Right, except the managers with whom you have a line relationship."

"What does this staff relationship do for me?"

"Staff relationships help you fulfill your accountability by giving you access to all the resources in the organizational resource bank. Managers are investment bankers. They decide where to invest their resources to get the highest rate of return for the organization. Let's look at the XYZ Company in its matrix structure again, and let's say you're the Director of Manufacturing.

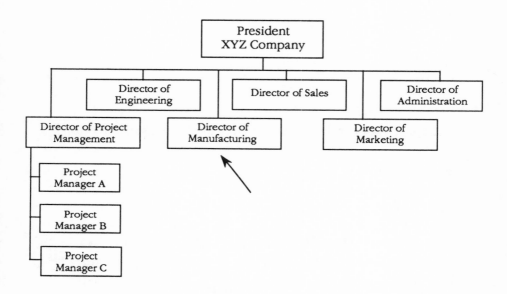

"Project Manager A needs widgets produced if she's going to fulfill her accountability, which, if you recall, is to meet profitability goals. She comes to you and describes her production requirements. You have several options: agree to her request, negotiate some changes in her request, or refuse her request. She wants you to invest your resources in her project. She is using a staff relationship to fulfill her accountability. She will also go to the other functional managers and request they use their resources to help her with her project."

"Investment bankers? That's an interesting analogy. What about more typical organizations, ones that don't use a matrix? Do they need staff relationships, too?"

"Yes. Let's discuss the 'typical' organization. We'll use XYZ again, without project management. You're the Director of Sales this time, so you're accountable for meeting a sales budget, right?"

"Right," I said.

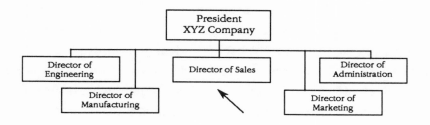

"In order to fulfill your accountability, you must have products to sell. You're depending on manufacturing to supply you with those products. You'll use a staff relationship to make sure those products are made and delivered so you can meet your budget. You'll use a staff relationship with engineering to make sure the the products being developed are ones your customers will buy. You'll use a staff relationship with marketing to make sure the marketing programs will help sell your products."

"I guess staff relationships are particularly important when accountability is defined as 'regardless of cause,'" I said. "A manager needs a mechanism to get help from other managers."

"Exactly. Every manager is given accountability for a piece of the common goal. Staff relationships provide the manager with access to *all* of the organization's resources to help him fulfill his goals."

"And, staff relationships are related to the internal customers and suppliers that we discussed at lunch?"

"Right. We said that internal suppliers were those groups or units that a manager depends on to fulfill his accountability, and internal customers were those groups who depend on him to fulfill their accountability. Staff relationships are the bridge to those other groups.

"The way to make the concept of internal customers and suppliers work is to first define areas of accountability and then define the specific accountabilities within each area. For each area, determine which groups the manager is most dependent on to fulfill his accountability. Those are his suppliers. He'd better be using his staff relationships to work closely with them so that they supply what he needs. Then he needs to look at which areas depend on him. They are his customers. He'll use his staff relationships to find out what they need so he can help them fulfill their accountability. Everyone is working together because they have an organizational accountability to do so, and, because they know they're all part of the same ship. It's all pretty simple, really."

"When you want to exercise a staff relationship, what level in the organization do you go to?"

"You go directly to the manager who has the resources you need."

"Doesn't bypassing the chain of command lead to chaos?"

"No. Accountability and the concept of only having one boss keep things in control. You simply go to the accountable manager for the area where you want something done. He will decide whether or not to invest his resources in what you want. If he accepts your proposal, he also accepts the accountability that goes with it. Accepting a new accountability might affect his ability to fulfill the accountability he already has. He'll need to take that up with his boss, but that's his concern, not yours."

"So, if I go to him and if he agrees to my proposal, it's up to him to work it out with his boss."

"Right. Of course, he might decide to discuss it with his boss before he agrees to your proposal, but again, that's up to him. You go to the accountable manager when you want to get something done."

"I like this stuff. Why is the staff relationship only available to managers? Can't specialists talk to managers?"

"Of course specialists can talk to managers. I'm not talking about limiting communication. A staff relationship, however, is not communication. It is a means of causing something to happen and making something happen is the role of the manager."

"Aren't staff relationships represented on organizational charts as dotted lines?"

"I'm not sure why people use dotted lines. If you have a staff relationship with every other manager in the organization, why have a dotted line to one or two of those managers? Maybe dotted lines are used because people don't understand the concept of staff relationships."

"Maybe."

"Let's examine the Principles of staff relationships."

Staff Relationship Principle No. 1: A staff relationship is used to introduce proposals to any management sector and to employ constructive means to cause acceptance of those proposals.

"What does 'constructive means' mean?" I asked.

"It means to convince, argue or persuade. It could mean getting others to help you to influence someone to accept your proposal. Remember, there is no authority in a staff relationship. Your proposal does not have to be accepted by the other manager, so you'd better be positively convincing."

> **Staff Relationship Principle No. 2:** **The staff relationship can be initiated by any manager. When employing a staff relationship, the manager must respect line relationships and act in accordance with organizational goals (organizational accountability).**

I said, "A staff relationship is a relationship between managers. Therefore, it's available to all managers. A manager must act in accordance with organizational accountability; we've covered that. What does 'respect line relationships' mean?"

"Let's say your boss's boss has a proposal for your area. He cannot give you an order, because he's not your boss, but he can make a proposal to you under a staff relationship. He must, however, respect the line relationship he has with your boss and the line relationship you have with your boss, which means he should probably go through your boss before making a proposal to you."

"So, if my boss's boss asks me to do something, I don't need to do it?"

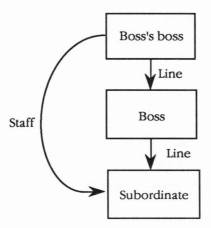

"Right. He's exercising a staff relationship so it's up to you to decide if you want to accept the proposal or not. If he wants to issue a direct order, he must go through your boss to do so."

"That's very interesting!" I said.

"Of course, it helps if the boss's boss understands the Kenning Principles before you refuse to do what he asks."

"So, getting back to respecting line relationships, are you saying that the boss's boss should use a line relationship to get something done at lower levels within his own unit?"

"Exactly. Although he is not precluded from going to lower levels in his own area, he shouldn't make a habit of it. Next Principle."

<u>Staff Relationship Principle No. 3</u>: The manager employing a staff relationship to make proposals is not accountable for the acceptance or implementation of his or her proposals.

"If manager X proposes to me that I do something, and I agree to do it, and it turns out to be a great success, then I'm accountable for the success. Right?" I asked.

"Right."

"What if manager X, who is an expert on a certain subject, gives me bad advice on that subject? I listen to him and the project fails. Isn't he accountable for his bad advice?"

"No. It was up to you to accept or not accept his advice."

"I think I'll get my advice somewhere else next time."

"That's certainly your option."

> **Staff Relationship Principle No. 4: Whether or not inputs provided through staff relationships are accepted is determined by the accountable manager receiving the inputs.**

"We just covered this. The manager receiving the proposal has the option of accepting or not accepting the proposal. If the proposal is accepted, then the accountability for the outcome goes with it."

"Right. Staff relationships cannot be used to transfer or get rid of accountability."

> **Staff Relationship Principle No. 5: Given healthy line relationships, staff relationships are the ingredient that enables an organization to function smoothly and effectively.**

"It seems staff relationships can be a big help in trying to fulfill one's accountability."

"Exactly. They form the managerial network of an organization. Staff relationships mean every manager is connected to every other manager. They flatten out any organization from a functional point of view. In effect, staff relationships mean there is no hierarchy when it comes to getting something done.

"That concludes our session for today. I'll add to the flow chart of what we've covered so far, and then we'll break. I'll see you in the morning for your final day."

I was ready for a break. I was exhausted.

THE ORGANIZATION:

*common goal
*specialization
*interdependence
*formal entity & under direction

*individual must not succeed at expense
 of the organization
*only as strong as weakest unit
*decisions made at lowest level possible

Organizational Structure:

*map of resources
*reporting relationships
*organize to fulfill common goal
*span of control = what can be
 effectively managed

Organizational Accountability:

*be of practical assistance in
 realization of organizational
 objectives
*required of all managers

ROLES IN AN ORGANIZATION:

SPECIALISTS:

*do the work

MANAGERS:

* direct the work
* make something planned happen through others
* make subordinates successful

Responsibility:

* do tasks & assignments
* fulfill job obligations

Role of Manager:

* management is direction
* effectiveness is not determined by job know-how
* can take over a number of
  diverse activities
* must preserve detached and
  nonpersonal relationships
* success depends on development and utilization of
  resources
* true value determined by
  contribution to success of
  others

Accountability:

* answer for results of
  others
* everything within area
* goals & objectives
* regardless of cause

Line Relationships:

* one boss
* set standards, review
  performance

Criteria:

* wants & likes position
* self-confident
* team player
* ethical standards

Staff Relationships:

* managers only
* introduce proposals
* network of an organi-
  zation

Day Three

The Role of the Specialist ————— 15

"Now that you understand the manager's role in the organization," the consultant said, "we need to discuss the role of the specialist. We said before that the specialist does the work of the organization. He produces things, does tasks. The work of the specialist moves the organization towards its goal."

"So the definition of a specialist is someone who does the work of the organization?"

"The complete definition of a specialist is:"

A specialist is the receiver of and fulfiller of specific responsibilities as delegated by his or her manager.

"If you recall," she said, "we defined responsibility as 'the fulfill-ment of specified tasks or assignments and satisfaction of job obliga-tions as delegated by a manager to a specialist.' We also said that delegation was 'the opportunity for the specialist to be of assistance in the fulfillment of a manager's accountability.' There is only one Prin-ciple of responsibility and it relates to delegation."

> **Responsibility Principle No. 1**: **Delegation is not to give away, to get rid of, to clear the desks with the thought that the work or problem will go away. It is not to unload, to unburden, to escape accountability. Delegation is not an opportunity to determine who is to be blamed for a failure.**

She continued, "What I want to make clear is that the specialist is not a scapegoat. The specialist does what he has been directed to do by the manager, and it's the manager who must account for the results. If there is a failure in the results, then the problem is with the manager, not with the specialist. The manager cannot turn around and blame a failure on the specialist, since the specialist does only what the man-ager directs him to do. It is up to the manager to ensure that the specialist is successful."

"Are you saying a specialist can do no wrong?" I asked.

"Almost. If there is a failure, it is a failure to train, to develop, to instruct and direct, to provide resources, or to otherwise cause the specialist to be successful. We are not going to let the first line man-ager use the specialist as an excuse or scapegoat for failure."

"So, if I am a first line supervisor, and one of my specialists screws up, I can't turn around and point to him and say, 'It's your fault.' I have to point to myself and ask, 'Where did I fail? What did I do that did not allow this person to be successful?'"

"Exactly."

"You're not saying that a specialist will never be fired."

"No. But, it's a last resort, and it represents a failure of accountability on the part of the manager. Most specialists can contribute effectively to the organization, if their managers will let them."

"Won't this kind of approach lead to specialists who think that all they have to do is sit back and wait for their bosses to tell them what to do?"

"I don't think so. It will lead to managers who realize that they really do have to manage. That's their job. What is so horrible about taking direction, anyway? An organization needs specialists who do what they've been asked to do. If you're a specialist, you must fulfill the job assignment delegated to you by your manager. Maybe you and your manager have discussed the nature of the assignment ahead of time; maybe you haven't. Your manager has told you what tasks he wants you to do. The degree of detail he gives you about how to do the tasks will depend on the nature of the task assignment and the abilities and training you have as a specialist. If you're an experienced, expert specialist, your manager may give you complete freedom on how to do the tasks. If you're inexperienced, his directions might be very specific. Regardless of how the direction is given, it is the specialist's job to do the tasks assigned to him by the manager."

"Somehow that sounds too easy."

"It should be 'easy.' The specialist should be free of concerns other than those related to actually getting the work done.

"Let's try some Specialist Principles."

Specialist Principle No. 1: The specialist must fulfill his or her work assignment.

"This Principle seems like common sense. The organization depends on the work done by specialists, so it's their job to do the tasks assigned."

"Right."

Specialist Principle No. 2: The specialist must recognize the manager as the person who provides direction and assistance in fulfilling the specialist's work assignment.

"I guess you're saying the specialist should understand the role of the manager," I said.

"That's right. If the specialist knows that the manager is supposed to provide direction and that the specialist is supposed to do the work assignment, there should be no misunderstanding about what is expected. Of course, if specialists understood what the manager's role was supposed to be, they might demand that managers actually fulfill that role. That would be something!"

Specialist Principle No. 3: The specialist must recognize the manager's accountability for what happens in the specific work area.

"This is basically the same as the last Principle, except that it addresses accountability instead of direction."

"Right. The specialist must understand that the manager is going to answer for or account for whatever happens within the manager's area of activity. The specialist should also understand that accountability is not concerned with blame or cause, which eliminates the potential of his being used as an excuse for failure. The specialist will understand that it's in the manager's best interest to ensure that the specialist is successful. So, an understanding of accountability ought to act as a beneficial ingredient in the manager/specialist relationship."

"Can you explain to me, one more time, why the specialist isn't accountable?"

"Simply speaking, accountability means that you answer for the results of others, whether subordinates or peers. The specialist doesn't work through others, so he cannot answer for the results of others."

"Yes, but don't you want specialists doing everything they can to get the job done, including utilizing other resources within the organization?"

"Now that you understand the role of the manager and the burden that accountability places on a manager, it ought to be clear that if the specialist also had to worry about fulfilling accountability, he would have less time to do the work, and work is the lifeblood of the organization.

"In addition, if you were to assign an area of accountability to a specialist, you would lose flexibility. The resource bank would become very structured and rigid. It would be difficult to shift resources quickly when tasks requirements change."

"Let me propose, then," I said, "that you change the definition of accountability for the specialist, and that you don't give him an area, and you don't make him accountable for the results of others. You merely make him accountable for his own results."

"But, his results are dependent on what others do. Remember interdependence?"

"Of course."

"Since the specialist's results are dependent on others, you can't give him accountability without giving him the opportunity to manage his interdependence. He would need to be able to negotiate his goals and objectives and make sure they were in line with organizational objectives, negotiate for resources, exercise staff relationships, etc. You're probably thinking this doesn't sound so bad. But, who is going to do the work while the specialist is spending all his time getting what he needs to fulfill the accountability you've given him? You would be making the specialist into a manager, and the skills required to be a manager are not the same as the skills required to be a specialist. So, rather than enhancing his specialist skills, you've spent your time and money training him on how to be a manager.

"Just for a minute, imagine what it would be like to be a specialist in an organization where the managers actually managed: where they provided clear direction, set fair and rational performance standards, and provided frequent feedback on the achievement of the standards. Imagine that the resources you needed to do your job were provided for you. Imagine that someone made sure that you were properly trained, and when you were trained, you were left you alone to do the tasks the organization had prepared you to do. Do you think a specialist in that situation is going to be lazy because he's not accountable?"

"No, probably not."

"He'd probably be delighted not to have to do his own job and the manager's job as well. It ought to be a nice change for him."

"You're pretty tough on management."

"That's because most managers don't manage. If they did, a lot of the concern about lazy, uncommitted specialists would go away. The burden of accountability is placed on the manager so the specialist will be free to do the work. It's time managers started doing their jobs and let the specialists do theirs. End of speech. Let's move on."

Specialist Principle No. 4: The specialist must recognize that the manager might designate certain qualified personnel (manager or specialist) to assist the specialist in the accomplishments of the specialist's job.

"So a manager might assign someone to help train or assist a specialist on an assignment?"

"That's right."

Specialist Principle No. 5: The specialist must appreciate and accept that decisions are made for the common organizational good.

"This says the specialist needs to understand the organizational goals."

"Not exactly. Although, the specialist should understand the overall goals and direction of the organization, he doesn't need to understand every organizational objective in order to do his job."

"Wait a minute. I think it's important for the specialist to under-stand all the organizational objectives. That way he feels a part of the team."

"I don't disagree that it can be helpful for the specialist to under-stand organizational objectives. I'm certainly not trying to discourage that. But, the specialist must do the assignment delegated to him, whether or not he understands how it fits into the larger picture, and whether or not he understands the reasons behind the decision. What the specialist must understand is that the manager is being held ac-countable for the assignment, and it is the accountability of the man-ager to make sure the assignment is consistent with organizational goals. It's the manager's job to worry about the big picture, not the specialist's.

"I'm not trying to cut the specialist out of the picture, I'm just trying to make sure his focus is on the work - how to do it, how to do it better - not on directing the organization."

"Okay. That makes sense," I said.

> **Specialist Principle No. 6: The specialist must have the freedom to contact other managerial personnel as required by his or her job assign-ment or as an alternate line of communication regarding his or her employment status.**

I considered this for a minute. "Well, we already said that special-ists could talk to managers in the organization if they wanted to."

"Right. This Principle also says the specialist has recourse if he cannot resolve problems with his boss. The specialist is dependent on his boss for direction, resources, work assignments, performance standards, performance evaluations, etc. The specialist must have the option of getting help from another manager if there is a problem with the boss/subordinate relationship. This is not a license to go around the manager on every decision. However, the specialist cannot be a prisoner of a manager. He must be free to contact others within the organization to resolve problems. And, it is up to the specialist to decide who he wants to contact."

"I agree with that."

"The manager/specialist relationship is one that should be built on mutual trust. When both parties fulfill their separate roles, the relationship between managers and specialists should be productive, satisfying and rewarding."

"So, you really think that if managers just did what they were supposed to do, specialists would be motivated, satisfied and productive workers?"

"Most of them would, yes. If you pick good people, train them well, trust them, tell them what you expect, evaluate them fairly - in other words be a good manager - then you'll see the true potential of the specialist emerge. The problem and the solution is management."

The Manager-to-Specialist Relationship   16

"We talked about line relationships yesterday. There are two kinds of line relationships: the line relationship between a specialist and a manager and the line relationship between two managers. Let's talk about the manager-to-specialist relationship first.

"The manager-to-specialist relationship is unique because the manager and the specialist have different roles in the organization. As we discussed yesterday, the management levels above the first line manager should be focused downward, so that the whole management team supports the manager-to-specialist interface."

"This seemed like an upside down view of management yesterday," I said, "but now it makes more sense to me than having everyone trying to please the top guy."

"I think so. Now that you're an expert on both the role of the specialist and the role of the manager, you shouldn't have any trouble explaining the Manager-to-Specialist Principles."

Manager-to-Specialist Principle No. 1: The manager is accountable for the success of the specialist.

"One of the ways a manager fulfills his accountability is by delegating responsibility to the specialist. If the specialist is successful at doing the work, then the manager is successful at fulfilling his accountability," I said.

"Right. The manager needs to provide the specialist everything he needs to do a task successfully. Then he needs to let the specialist do the task."

Manager-to-Specialist Principle No. 2: The manager must establish appropriate criteria for selection of the specialist and must pick the right person. The lack of qualified personnel is the result of an ineffective manager.

"Are there criteria for specialists?"

"The Principles don't outline any criteria for specialists, but that doesn't mean you shouldn't develop a list of your own."

"I think I'll do that with my new management team. One of the items on the list ought to be attention to detail."

"Good idea," she said.

"The last sentence of Principle No. 2 means that it is up to the manager to ensure that the specialist is effective. If the specialist is

ineffective, then either the manager didn't pick the right person or he
didn't give him the help or direction he needed."

"I think you're going to pass this course."

"What if a manager takes over a new position, so that he inherits
the people in the group?"

"He's still accountable for them, and it's up to him to make them
successful."

"I thought so."

Manager-to-Specialist Principle No. 3: The manager must establish rational performance standards for the work to be done in his or her area of accountability.

"The specialist should know what is expected of him in the job;
that would be the performance standards. He is being paid to do a job,
and he should know what constitutes fulfilling that obligation to the
organization. It also says the standards of performance must be rational and fair."

"Excellent."

Manager-to-Specialist Principle No. 4: The manager must give orders or instructions that are fair, honest, safe, and that satisfy fixed perform-ance standards in an understandable manner.

"I like this Principle. It says a manager has to treat the specialist fairly, honestly and safely. It also says the manager must give instructions that are understandable. It's not enough to tell someone to do something. He must understand what you are telling him to do. The burden is on the manager to be clear about what is expected."

Manager-to-Specialist Principle No. 5: The manager must ensure that assignments are well-directed.

"This says almost the same thing as the last Principle. Make sure the assignment is clear and in line with organizational and functional objectives."

"Right."

Manager-to-Specialist Principle No. 6: The manager must maximize the capabilities (potential) of the specialist within the organization. An ineffective subordinate is the product of an ineffective manager.

"This says that the manager must utilize the potential of the specialist, which means first knowing him well enough so that you know what his potential is. Then, it would mean asking his advice, getting his inputs, etc. I think we could make better use of the specialists' talents at Global than we do."

"Don't feel bad. That's true for most organizations. This is an important Principle because it reinforces the role of the specialist as the doer and the role of the manager as the director. It says the manager must make the most of the human resources under his care."

Manager-to-Specialist Principle No. 7: The manager must provide the necessary resources for the specialist to fulfill the job requirements.

"The specialist can't fulfill the job requirements without the resources required to do the job. It's the job of the manager to provide the resources."

"Right, and if the manager doesn't know what resources the specialist needs, all he has to do is ask."

Manager-to-Specialist Principle No. 8: The manager must evaluate the performance of the specialist in a nonprejudicial manner.

"This goes back to the manager being objective. A manager must evaluate the performance of a specialist based on the preset performance standards, not based on non-job related issues."

"Very good."

Manager-to-Specialist Principle No. 9: **The manager must maximize the use of the specialist's expertise when arriving at decisions or work orders.**

"The specialist should be used as a resource to the organization. He has expertise that is of value, and it should be utilized when the manager makes a decision or gives work orders."

"Right. Not availing oneself of the expertise of the specialist is a mismanagement of resources."

Manager-to-Specialist Principle No. 10: **The manager must maintain relationships or working conditions that are conducive to effective fulfillment of job requirements.**

"All this says is that the manager has to make sure the specialist has what he needs to do his job. Part of what he needs is an objective, nonprejudicial boss and decent working conditions. Nothing too radical in that," I said.

Manager-to-Specialist Principle No. 11: **The manager must be aware of and address the external factors that might unduly influence the specialist's job performance.**

"I'm not sure what external factors you're referring to."

"For example, if a manager's boss is disturbing his specialists, it is up to the manager to use corrective action upward to rectify the situation. It is not the specialist's job to correct the boss's boss or other outside factors that affect his job performance."

"Corrective action upward?"

"Yes. You must correct your boss if he does something that interferes with your ability to fulfill your accountability."

"That's an interesting concept."

Manager-to-Specialist Principle No. 12: The manager must inform the specialist that contacts outside the manager are available.

"We said earlier that the specialist needs to have an avenue of redress if irresolvable differences arise between the manager and the specialist. So, this says that it's up to the manager to make it clear to the specialist that he is free to avail himself of outside contacts, if needed."

"Exactly."

Manager-to-Specialist Principle No. 13: The manager must personally take corrective action as required to maintain performance standards.

"So the manager is the person who provides feedback to the specialist."

"Right. It means that the manager can't send a specialist to personnel to be corrected. And, correction is only concerned with maintaining the standards that have been set ahead of time. The subordinate needs frequent, personal feedback on how he's doing.

"It's like setting a thermostat. You have a target temperature, such as 70 degrees. If you set the range too wide, say plus or minus ten degrees, it gets very cold before the heat kicks on. You have deviated too far from your target. But, if you set it for plus or minus two degrees, the actual temperature will always be close to your target temperature. The same is true of performance. Provide frequent feedback so that performance is always right on target."

Manager-to-Specialist Principle No. 14: The manager must take into consideration the impact on the specialist's well-being when changing the specialist's employment status.

"What does 'well-being' mean?"

"Well-being includes such things as income potential, mental health, physical health, utilization of the specialist's skills, etc."

"So you can't change specialists' jobs without considering what the repercussions are."

"Right."

Manager-to-Specialist Principle No. 15: The manager must represent all organizational policies as his or her own.

"I think I'm stuck. Does this mean that if something is a personnel policy, that I have to pretend it's my policy?"

"Not pretend. It *is* your policy. Every manager is an author of organizational policies. Policies are put together for the benefit of the organization. Remember we said that organizations don't make decisions; individuals make decisions. So organizational policies are policies decided on by an individual for the good of the organization.

"You are the organization to your specialists, and you must support the organizational policies as if they were authored by you. If a policy does not help you fulfill your accountability, then you need to get it changed. You cannot say, 'Personnel came up with this salary policy. I'd really like to give you more money, but my hands are tied.' The salary policy *is* your policy."

"This is going to take some getting used to. You're saying I have to buy-in to every policy or else get it changed. I can't pass the buck, ever?"

"No. You are the representive of the organization to your people."

"I can see the logic of it, but practice could be another matter. Does this hold true for the line relationship between managers as well?"

"Of course."

The Manager-to-Manager Relationship 17

"We're heading into the home stretch. Are the Principles making sense to you?" she asked.

"Things are falling into place. I can see the value of everyone operating under these Principles, but, if my crew is the only group in the organization following them, how does that work?"

"It is true that the more people in an organization who follow the Principles, the more effective they will be. But, if you and your crew set an example for the others, maybe you'll start to attract some attention. The rest of the organization will want to know what your secret is."

"Yes. I guess you have to start somewhere. Changing an entire organization takes time."

"Not only time, but commitment. Putting these Principles into action requires constant attention and practice. You don't change overnight."

"That's true."

"Let's move on so that you can get back and start practicing. When discussing the line relationship between managers, we're going to call one manager the boss and the other manager the subordinate. The first six Principles of the Manager-to-Manager Relationship refer to the boss. These should be a snap."

Manager-to-Manager Principle No. 1: Boss is accountable for the success of the subordinate.

"A manager is accountable for the resources he has been given, which in this case, would be the managers who report to him. So, he is accountable for making them successful."

"This Principle," she said, "like the similar one covered under the Manager-to-Specialist Principles, is one of the key Principles, which is why it is included as one of the Cardinal Rules."

"Cardinal Rules?"

"Yes, the ten major Principles, but we'll get to them later. Let's keep going."

Manager-to-Manager Principle No. 2: Boss must establish appropriate criteria for selection of subordinates and must pick the right person. The lack of qualified personnel is the result of an ineffective manager.

"This is just like the Manager-to-Specialist Principle. You must have a common set of criteria for managers. It also says that if you have ineffective people, you're an ineffective manager, whether you picked the people or inherited them."

"Right."

"Doesn't anyone ever get fired?"

"Of course. The manager is accountable for the success of his people. If they fail, he fails. If one of them continues to fail and the manager cannot cause that person to be successful, he may have to fire the person. But, when you have to fire someone, you have failed in your accountability. Of course keeping someone who can't contribute to the organization would be a larger failure."

"I see," I replied. I could understand that you wouldn't want to fire people indiscriminately, and that you would have to do everything possible to make them successful, but sometimes you just have to let people go. I had always felt like a failure when I had to fire someone, but keeping them always seemed worse.

Manager-to-Manager Principle No. 3: Boss must define subordinate's area of accountability and provide direction that is consistent with organizational objectives.

"I thought we said in an earlier Principle that it was the subordinate who had to make sure he knew what his area of accountability was."

"That true. The subordinate doesn't get off the hook if he doesn't know what the boundaries of his area are. However, since the boss must help the subordinate succeed, the boss needs to make certain the subordinate does know what he's accountable for. In addition, the boss must provide clear direction that is in line with the goals of the organization."

"Okay. That makes sense."

Manager-to-Manager Principle No. 4: Boss must give subordinate the authorities as required to satisfy the assigned accountability.

"This must be similar to the last Principle. Although the subordinate must be able to manage without direct authority, the boss needs to make sure the subordinate has the authority needed to fulfill his accountability."

"Exactly."

Manager-to-Manager Principle No. 5: Boss must personally acknowledge performance in an appropriate line relationship.

"I guess this means you can't send your subordinate a note saying, 'You screwed up.'"

"That's one way to explain this Principle. The boss/subordinate relationship requires constant attention. Part of the function of the boss/subordinate relationship is to assign accountability and to evaluate the fulfillment of that accountability. This should be done personally by the boss and done frequently, not once a year. It's the concept of setting the thermostat that we talked about in the last section."

Manager-to-Manager Principle No. 6: Boss must direct performance acknowledgement to the specific area of accepted accountability.

"It seems to me that if you evaluate performance frequently, it will be easier to be specific about what is right and what is wrong, because you won't have a lot of things stored up that haven't been discussed."

"Right. Frequent feedback is paramount.

"Let's move on to what the subordinate manager must do to hold up his end of the boss/subordinate relationship."

Manager-to-Manager Principle No. 7: Subordinate owes boss an accounting for subordinate's area of accountability.

"This seems straightforward," I said. "The boss has entrusted an area of accountability to a subordinate, and the subordinate must account for what happened within that area."

Manager-to-Manager Principle No. 8: Subordinate must provide corrective action upward when boss's conduct disturbs subordinate's area of accountability.

"Here's that corrective action again. Well, after all, the boss isn't perfect."

"Since the boss wants to make the subordinate successful, he also needs feedback. If the organization has chosen its managers according to the manager criteria we discussed yesterday, managers should not have trouble with this Principle because they benefit from criticism, learn from others, etc. Corrective action upward would seem to them like a normal way of operating."

"I think that, at Global at least, it's the exception and not the rule."

"Again, it's a part of a healthy boss/subordinate relationship - a relationship that is interactive. A boss/subordinate relationship cannot be a one-way street."

Manager-to-Manager Principle No. 9: **Ultimately, a subordinate must agree with and support the position of his or her boss.**

I was confused by this Principle. "I think I'd like to hear your explanation of this one," I said.

"The subordinate is not a passive receptacle for whatever the boss asks. You remember we said that the boss and subordinate must agree on the goals, and if the boss and subordinate cannot agree, then the boss has the final say. When the subordinate accepts the boss's position, he also accept the accountability that goes with it. The boss's position becomes the subordinate's position, just like accepting organizational policies as one's own. If you can't buy in, then get it changed. If you don't get it changed, you automatically accept it."

"That's not so easy."

"I know, but think about it in the context of a boss/subordinate relationship that is built on mutual respect and trust. The relationship
has a give and take to it because both individuals are trying to pursue
the same goals, even if they have different views about how to go
about doing that. A subordinate is not a messenger. He and his boss
should discuss and debate important issues until agreement is
reached."

"What if the subordinate still isn't convinced?" I asked.

"He then has three options. He can continue to argue, and even get
others to help him argue, if appropriate. He can resign. Or, he can
accept the boss's decision and support it as his own. Most things
aren't important enough to fight to 'the death.' Some things are.
That's a matter of judgement."

Manager-to-Manager Principle No. 10: **Subordinate must be prepared to adjust arguments to
support boss.**

"This sounds like a corollary to the last Principle. So, if you
ultimately support the position of your boss, you have to be prepared
to argue the boss's position because theoretically, he's convinced you
he's right. You can't say, 'Well, I didn't agree, but my boss insisted.'
You've accepted it. It's yours, and you must represent it as your
own."

"Exactly."

Manager-to-Manager Principle No. 11: Subordinate can only be as good as his or her boss.

"I guess if the boss/subordinate relationship is working as you have described it, then the subordinate is going to depend heavily on the boss, and he's only going to be as successful as the boss is successful. If the boss gives poor direction, the subordinate will suffer. If the boss does not provide the needed resources, the subordinate will suffer. So the subordinate must help make sure that the boss is successful so that the subordinate can also be successful. Is that it?"

"That's it exactly. You've come a long way in two and a half days. Why don't you look over the Manager-to-Specialist and Manager-to-Manager Principles and see if there is anything you have a question on. We'll cover Manager Development, Organizational Accountability Principles and the Cardinal Rules after lunch."

THE MANAGER-TO-SPECIALIST RELATIONSHIP

1. The manager is accountable for the success of the specialist.

2. The manager must establish appropriate criteria for selection of the specialist and must pick the right person. The lack of qualified personnel is the result of an ineffective manager.

3. The manager must establish rational performance standards for the work to be done in his or her area of accountability.

4. The manager must give orders or instructions that are fair, honest, safe, and that satisfy fixed performance standards in an understandable manner.

5. The manager must ensure that assignments are well-directed.

6. The manager must maximize the capabilities (potential) of the specialist within the organization. An ineffective subordinate is the product of an ineffective manager.

7. The manager must provide the necessary resources for the specialist to fulfill the job requirements.

8. The manager must evaluate the performance of the specialist in a nonprejudicial manner.

9. The manager must maximize the use of the specialist's expertise when arriving at decisions or work orders.

10. The manager must maintain relationships or working conditions that are conducive to effective fulfillment of job requirements.

THE MANAGER-TO-MANAGER RELATIONSHIP

1. Boss is accountable for the success of the subordinate.

2. Boss must establish appropriate criteria for selection of subordinates and must pick the right person. The lack of qualified personnel is the result of an ineffective manager.

3. Boss must define subordinate's area of accountability and provide direction that is consistent with organizational objectives.

4. Boss must give subordinate the authorities as required to satisfy the assigned accountability.

5. Boss must personally acknowledge performance in an appropriate line relationship.

6. Boss must direct performance acknowledgement to the specific area of accepted accountability.

7. Subordinate owes boss an accounting for subordinate's area of accountability.

8. Subordinate must provide corrective action upward when boss's conduct disturbs subordinate's area of accountability.

9. Ultimately, a subordinate must agree with and support the position of his or her boss.

10. Subordinate must be prepared to adjust arguments to support boss.

11. Subordinate can only be as good as his or her boss.

THE MANAGER-TO-SPECIALIST RELATIONSHIP (CONT.)

11. The manager must be aware of and address the external factors that might unduly influence the specialist's job performance.

12. The manager must inform the specialist that contacts outside the manager are available.

13. The manager must personally take corrective action as required to maintain performance standards.

14. The manager must take into consideration the impact on the specialist's well-being when changing the specialist's employment status.

15. The manager must represent all organizational policies as his or her own.

Lunch
(The Consultant)

I was interested in learning how the consultant had gotten involved with the Kenning Principles in the first place. When lunch arrived, I asked her about it.

"I used to work for a large corporation," she said, "in one of their research divisions. George Kenning was a consultant for them. I took his course when I first joined the company. That was in 1981. I'd had previous management experience, but I'd never been exposed to anything like the Kenning Principles. I was stunned by what accountability really meant. Once I understood the concept, it propelled me into action. To me, the Principles described a dynamic process. I liked that. When I started applying the Principles, I got results. I attribute a large part of my managerial success to practicing the Principles."

"It's good to know they really do work."

"Oh, they work all right. Anyway, I used to help George with some of his courses, and we got to be friends. Then, he asked if I would write a book about the Principles. George and I, together with a gentleman named Robert Wilbur, began to work on a book project. We spent the first year developing the actual Principles. George had been using a set of '31 points,' as he called them, to explain his management philosophy. The three of us converted his philosophy into a complete set of Principles. When we completed writing the Principles, I started writing the book. Then, George died."

"When was that?" I asked.

"November, 1988. I put the book on hold for awhile and developed a course to teach the Principles instead."

"That's the *Back to Basics* course?"

"That's right. In July of 1989, I decided to take the plunge and to start my own business teaching the Kenning Principles."

"It seems you've been successful. Whatever happened to the book?"

"Oh, it's almost finished. I'll send you a copy when it's printed. I think you'll find it very interesting."

"I'm looking forward to it."

"Have you thought about how you're going to apply these Principles when you start your new assignment?" she asked.

"I think I'm going to set up a meeting with my management team before we ship out for our first cruise. We'll go through the Principles one-by-one, much like you have done. Hopefully, I'll get them right."

"That's a good way to start. Then everyone on your team will understand what the management process is all about. You'll share a common language and a common understanding of what management really means."

"Then, I thought maybe we'd work on defining areas of accountability. I would also like to define each group's internal customers and suppliers. That way we'll know where the major interdependencies are. Oh yes, we're also going to develop a list of criteria for specialists, and we need to see what we might want to add to the manager criteria list."

"Good idea."

"Finally, we'll need to outline specific objectives within each area. That ought to keep me busy for awhile."

"Yes, I think it will. It sounds like a good plan. We'd better go finish up so you can get back to Global and do some implementation."

Manager Development

18

"I'm eager to start using these Principles, so that I can develop myself as a manager."

"That just happens to be the subject of this section: management development."

"Funny how that keeps happening."

"Yes, isn't it? Management development is both an individual and an organizational effort. The Principles address those things that an organization needs to do to develop its managers. You remember how we went through manager criteria?"

I nodded that I did.

"We'll do the same here. I'll explain the general categories and you can explain the specific development activities within each category."

"No problem," I said.

A. The Job

"You can study management all you want, but there's no substitute for actually managing," she said. "The job itself contains components or activities that help a manager develop."

1. Position descriptions

"Let's see," I said. "A position description for a manager outlines his area of accountability. That way he knows what he's accountable for."

"Exactly. By defining the limits or boundaries of the job, the manager begins to know what is expected of him."

2. Performance standards

"Performance standards are the goals or objectives within an area of accountability. A combination of the performance standards and the position description ought to give a manager a complete understanding of the expectations of the job."

"You're pretty good at this."

3. Evaluation systems

"Evaluation systems measure whether or not you have achieved that which was expected - have you met the performance standards?"

"Right. Evaluation systems tell the manager how he is doing. They are a feedback mechanism that help a manager monitor his performance."

4. Wage and salary structures

"This is another, very concrete, feedback system. It rewards performance," I said.

"Right. Wage and salary structures should reward managers who fulfill their accountability, thus providing an incentive for the acceptance of accountability."

5. Boss/subordinate relationships

"It has become apparent to me that the boss is critical to the development of a subordinate. He provides guidance, counsel and support in helping the subordinate fulfill his accountability. He sets the performance standards, and he evaluates the performance. He administers the wage and salary system."

"The subordinate can also help in the boss's development," she said. "The subordinate provides corrective action upward which is an additional feedback system for the boss.

"In order to develop as a manager, you must understand the organization within which you work."

B. The Organization

She explained, "The organization should provide activities that help a manager understand the organizational objectives and help him utilize the resources of the organization."

1. Staff meetings

"Although I have been known to complain about staff meetings at times, it seems that they can help a manager develop staff relationships. They can also help him understand the 'big picture.'"

"Excellent."

2. Organizational models

"The organizational model or chart outlines the resources of the organization. It should also tell a manager who is accountable for what so that staff relationships can be more easily initiated."

"As you expressed it the first day, it's the organization's road map, and without it a manager can get lost. It also helps provide the big picture."

3. Fixed manager criteria

"I really like the idea of having a common or fixed set of manager criteria that everyone in the organization adheres to. It can help serve as a guidepost for what the organization is looking for in its managers. An individual could compare his own strengths and weaknesses to the criteria, and that would guide him in his development activities."

4. Skill inventories

"This is a new one. Do you mean the how-to's?" I asked.

"Yes. Just because the Principles address the *what* and not the *how*, doesn't mean the *how* isn't important. Skills required to do the manager's job might include communicating, planning, organizing, etc. Skill inventories are another form of feedback. What skills are needed to be a good manager? Which skills do I have? Which ones do I need to improve?"

5. Management training

"What I think you said before was that training is only one aspect of development."

"That's exactly what I said. Management training primarily addresses skill improvement, and it is merely a tool to assist the development process. It cannot replace it.

"The next category is the management experience."

C. The Experience

"There are management experiences which help broaden and develop a manager so that he learns the profession of managing," she said.

1. Special assignments

"I take it you mean some kind of additional assignment?" I asked.

"Right. They are added accountabilities for short periods of time."

"I can see that they could help develop your managerial capabilities, particularly if you have been in one position for long time."

"A special assignment is one way to develop a manager that does not require a promotion. Experience exchange is another."

2. Experience exchange

"I take it this means a lateral move."

"Yes," she said.

"I can see where a lateral move is beneficial in expanding the managerial experience. Essentially, that's what I'm doing. It can provide new tests to your managerial capabilities, and it should teach you to manage a number of diverse activities - wasn't that the wording of one of the Principles?"

"Right. New accountabilities, either temporary, as in special assignments, or permanent, as in experience exchanges, force a manager to manage. However, new accountabilities cannot be given out haphazardly. Managers must be carefully selected for new assignments, and the organization must be prepared to provide additional support and counsel to the manager who takes on the new assignment.

Throwing someone into the ocean without a life jacket is not management development. Unfortunately, all too often that's what happens."

"Let's not talk about drowning in the ocean, if you don't mind."

"Sorry."

D. The Opportunity: Promotion from Within

She continued, "Promotion from within is the opportunity for managers to take on broader areas of accountability. It is concrete evidence that an organization is serious about developing managers. It represents an incentive for managerial development. Anytime an organization goes outside to find a manager, a failure has occurred. An organization that is serious about promotion from within is also serious about management development.

"That completes the list. There is only one Principle of Management Development:"

> **Manager Development Principle No. 1**: **An organization can never cause anyone to become a manager. Assistance and opportunity for such progression can be afforded, but the desire, effort, and accountability for betterment as a manager must be within the person concerned.**

"This says that although an organization should assist the manager and provide him opportunities for development, in the end, it is up to the individual to develop himself as a manager," I said.

"Exactly. Not only is the manager accountable for developing his subordinates, but he is accountable for developing himself as well."

"Accountability is everywhere, isn't it?"

"You noticed, huh? Take a minute to review the management development list and then we'll move on to the last set of new Principles."

Categories	**Activities**
A. The Job	1. position descriptions
	2. performance standards
	3. evaluation systems
	4. wage and salary structures
	5. boss/subordinate relationships
B. The Organization	1. staff meetings
	2. organization models
	3. fixed manager criteria
	4. skill inventories
	5. management training
C. The Experience	1. special assignments
	2. experience exchange
D. The Opportunity	1. promotion from within

Organizational Accountability Principles ___ 19

"I left the Principles of Organizational Accountability until last because they readdress the relationship of the manager to the organization, which I think is a good place to end. So, let's see what you've learned."

Organizational Accountability Principle No. 1: A manager must identify with and support all organizational goals.

"I have to admit I wouldn't have accepted this Principle when I walked in the door two days ago, but it seems quite reasonable now. The manager is the author of organizational goals. He sets goals for his group, consistent with the organizational goals. Here, let me diagram it for you." I stood up and grabbed a magic marker. The consultant smiled.

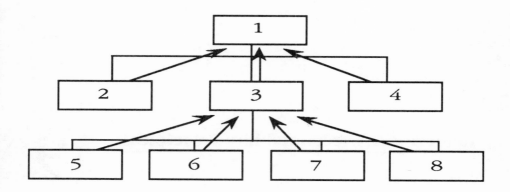

"If No. 1 sets the overall goals for the organization, then numbers 2, 3, and 4 must accept those goals or get Number 1 to change them. Once they accept the goals, they set the goals for their areas in support of the organization's goals. Numbers 5, 6, 7, and 8 do the same thing with Number 3's goals. The goals then get broken down into smaller and smaller chunks, each supporting the larger organizational goals. That way everyone is a part of the same team, going in the same direction."

She clapped. I put down the magic marker, bowed slightly, and sat down.

"You've gotten so good, the next Principle should be a snap," she said.

Organizational Accountability Principle No. 2: A manager must demonstrate absolute loyalty to the organization.

I frowned as I looked at Principle No. 2. Absolute loyalty? "I'm having trouble with this one," I said. "I don't understand where loyalty fits in."

"The manager's role is to take care of the organizational good. He has been given resources to use to further the organizational good. He has been given accountability that must be discharged for the overall good. So, as long as the manager is part of an organization, he owes the organization his commitment to act in its behalf. That is what loyalty means. If he finds he can't do that, he'd better leave.

"Loyalty doesn't mean doing something illegal or immoral for the organization. That isn't in the organization's best interest. And, hopefully, by now you understand that management is not about blindly following orders. The manager represents the organization's interests. Therefore, he and the organization are one."

"I see what you mean. Yes, I guess I can buy that."

<u>Organizational Accountability Principle No. 3</u>: All management members share authorship of organizational policies, procedures, and practices.

"Well, this one I can handle, since we've discussed it before. Managers set the policies, procedures, and practices, just as they set the goals of an organization, and so, theoretically they share authorship of those policies and procedures, even if they didn't write the policies themselves. When they implement them, they must represent them as if they were their own. That was a Principle, as I recall. If they can't support them as their own, they'd better get them changed."

"By gosh, I think you've got it."

Organizational Accountability Principle No. 4:
Policies, procedures, and practices are only as
meaningful as the capabilities of the managers
applying them.

"This is pretty self-evident. Policies, procedures and practices are something on a piece of paper. They have to be implemented by managers; therefore, they will be as effective as the managers who implement them."

"Right. Managers are what bring policies to life.

"Well, that brings us to the last Principle," she said.

"How sad."

Organizational Accountability Principle No. 5:
Any status change of the manager is to be
accepted as beneficial to the best interest of the
organization.

I considered this last Principle before I spoke, partly because it was the last Principle and partly because I was having trouble interpreting it.

"I'm going to give this my best shot," I said. "You get promoted because it is in the best interest of the organization to do so. If you receive a lateral move, an experience exchange, it's because it is in the best interest of the organization. And, as I recall, individual interests cannot take precedence over organizational interests. So, if you get demoted, then it's because it's in the best interest of the organization.

A manager has to accept that changes in status are made because it is in the best interest of the organization to do so."

"Perfect. When the organizational interest is served, you are also served, since you depend on the health of the organization. If a status change occurs, it's for the survival, growth, and health of the organization. Managers have to accept that changes in status are made for the good of the organization, not for the good of the individual.

"That concludes the Principles. Since there are so many Principles, they've been boiled down to a set of Cardinal Rules. We'll cover those quickly in the last section. But first, let me finish the flow chart of what we've covered over the past three days."

THE ORGANIZATION:

- common goal
- specialization
- interdependence
- formal entity & under direction
- individual must not succeed at expense of the organization
- only as strong as weakest unit
- decisions made at lowest level possible

Organizational Structure:

- map of resources
- reporting relationships
- organize to fulfill common goal
- span of control = what can be effectively managed

Organizational Accountability:

- be of practical assistance in realization of organizational objectives
- required of all managers

ROLES IN AN ORGANIZATION:

SPECIALISTS:

- do the work

Responsibility:

- do tasks & assignments
- fulfill job obligations

MANAGERS:

- direct the work
- make something planned happen through others
- make subordinates successful
- maximize the use of others
- identify with and support all organizational goals
- share authorship of organizational policies

Role of Specialist:

- fulfill work assignment
- recognize manager's accountabilty
- appreciate decisions are for common good
- free to contact other managers if needed

Role of Manager:

- management is direction
- effectiveness is not determined by job know-how
- can take over a number of diverse activities
- must preserve detached and nonpersonal relationships
- success depends on development and utilization of resources
- true value determined by contribution to success of others

Accountability:

- answer for results of others
- everything within area
- goals & objectives
- regardless of cause

Line Relationships:

- one boss
- set standards, review performance

Staff Relationships:

- managers only
- introduce proposals
- network of an organization

Criteria:

- wants & likes position
- self-confident
- team player
- ethical standards

Development:

- the job
- the organization
- the experience
- the opportunity

The Cardinal Rules

20

"The Ten Cardinal Rules of Management summarize the key points of the Kenning Principles."

1. All members of an organization are interdependent.
2. Management is direction.
3. A manager is someone who is accountable for making something planned happen.
4. Acceptance of accountability is the key factor in determining whether a manager is a manager.
5. Acceptance of accountability must be complete and without qualification.
6. Success as a manager depends upon the manager's ability to utilize available resources.
7. The manager is accountable for the success of his or her subordinates (if the manager has subordinates).
8. A manager must identify with and support all organizational goals.
9. Decisions should be made at the lowest level possible.
10. A manager is someone who wants and likes the manager's job, who has a strong sense of self, who is a team player, and who has a set of internalized moral standards.

"The Cardinal Rules summarize what we've covered in The Kenning Principles. The first Rule says, 'All members of an organization are interdependent.' Interdependence, if you recall, is on of the basic characteristics of an organization and a major part of the foundation of the Principles, since interdependence is what ties everyone in an organization together, thus creating the whole.

"We also said that an organization is under direction and managers are the directors of an organization. As the second Rule says, 'Management is direction.'

"The third Rule which says, 'A manager is someone who is accountable for making something happen,' is really just a part of the definition of a manager. Making something happen is important if the organization is going to reach its goals, and goals are why the organization exists in the first place.

"Of course, the Cardinal Rules wouldn't be complete without a dose of accountability. Rules four and five deal with acceptance of accountability by the manager. I think you now have an appreciation of what acceptance of accountability means. Accountability is a burden and a challenge, and it is what characterizes the manager's job.

"We also stressed that management is about utilizing others and making those others successful. The sixth and seventh Rules emphasize these points.

"Rule number eight says, 'A manager must identify with and support all organizational goals.' We know that this is one of the Principles of organizational accountability. It emphasizes the need for every manager to take care of the whole.

"Rule number nine says, 'Decisions should be made at the lowest level possible.' We covered that in the first section on the organization. Decision making should be pushed down so that a decision and the corresponding responsibility or accountability are at the same level. Specialists generally make decisions about how-to-do something and managers generally make decisions about what-to-do.

"The last Cardinal Rule summarizes the criteria for managers. Managers must be able to accept accountability; they must be part of the team but also able to stand alone, and they have to act in accordance with internal ethical standards.

"That's it. Hopefully the Cardinal Rules will be a quick reminder of the key concepts of the Kenning Principles."

"I think so," I said, "although I can't quite imagine that I'm going to forget them."

"I hope not. Well, congratulations! You've learned the Kenning Principles."

"These Principles have unlocked the secrets of management for me. I now understand what management is really all about, and I finally feel like I am standing on firm ground when it comes to managing."

"Great. Do you think that what you've learned will cause you to change the way you manage?" she asked.

"Definitely. I realize I have to depend more on my crew. Applying the concept of accountability will certainly mean I'll do some things differently, such as spending more time developing and supporting my people than I used to."

"When you focus on helping your people realize their potential," she said, "I think you'll be surprised at what they'll achieve. When you appeal to what they can be, they will become what you expect. Give your managers accountability and then support their efforts to fulfill that accountability. It sounds like you are on the road to developing an excellent organization."

"I'm certainly going to work hard at it."

"That's exactly what it takes. Constant drill and hard work. Understanding the Principles is easy. Applying them is the hard part."

I knew these Principles wouldn't guarantee my success, but I also knew they'd help me be successful if I worked at them. I no longer felt there was something about management I was missing. Now all I had to do was implement what I had learned.

"Good luck on your new assignment," she said as I was leaving. "Let me know how things work out."

"Oh, you'll definitely hear from me," I said. "And, thanks again."

Appendix

Appendix Table of Contents

THE ORGANIZATION   Page Ref.

An **organization** is a formal entity, consisting of an interdependent   22
group of people, working together, under direction, toward a
common goal.

1. All members of an organization must act for the organizational   26
good. Therefore, an individual must not succeed at the expense of
the organization.

2. Organizational functioning is the result of each member of the   27
organization fulfilling his or her role within the organization.
Every member of an organization is equally important.

3. Organizational efficiency is produced through units working   28
together interdependently and cohesively. An organization is only
as good as its least effective unit.

4. As an entity, an organization does not make decisions, but does   29
provide a framework within which decisions can be made in an
orderly manner.

5. Decisions should be made at the lowest level possible.   30

ORGANIZATIONAL STRUCTURE

ACCOUNTABILITY

Accountability is the recognition and acceptance that one is answerable for whatever happens within an area of activity, regardless of cause. Accountability is exclusive to the management function.

1. Acceptance of accountability is the key factor in determining if a manager is a manager.

2. An area of accountability must be defined. It might be defined by one's immediate superior, or, if not, the limits must be sought.

3. Acceptance of accountability must be complete and without qualification.

4. Accountability is not shared; neither is authority.

5. Fulfillment of accountability is the basis upon which a manager's performance is evaluated.

RESPONSIBILITY   Page Ref.

Responsibility is the fulfillment of specified tasks or assignments   55
and satisfaction of job obligations as delegated by a manager (boss)
to a specialist (subordinate).

Delegation is the creation of an opportunity for a specialist to be of   56
assistance in the fulfillment of a manager's accountability. A
manager delegates responsibility to a specialist, but retains accountability.

1. Delegation is not to give away, to get rid of, to clear the desks   134
with the thought that the work or problem will go away. It is not to
unload, to unburden, to escape accountability. Delegation is not an
opportunity to determine who is to be blamed for a failure.

ORGANIZATIONAL ACCOUNTABILITY

Organizational accountability, the accountability to be of practical
assistance in the realization of any organizational objectives, is
required of all managers.

1. A manager must identify with and support all organizational
goals.

2. A manager must demonstrate absolute loyalty to the organization.

3. All management members share authorship of organizational
policies, procedures, and practices.

4. Policies, procedures, and practices are only as meaningful as the
capabilities of the managers applying them.

5. Any status change of the manager is to be accepted as beneficial
to the best interest of the organization.

THE ROLE OF THE MANAGER   Page Ref.

A **manager** is someone who is accountable for making something   75
planned happen within a specific area through the use of available
resources. Management is direction; it is neither consensus nor
example.

1. Only a manager has accountability. The burden of accountabil-   79
ity distinguishes the manager from the specialist.

2. Each manager position should be recognized within an organ-   80
izational structure and should include a specific area of accountability, authority or not, subordinates or not.

3. Functional accountability notwithstanding, each manager bears   84
an organizational accountability that recognizes the essential tenet
for having an organization in the first place - a common goal. A
manager, therefore, must take care of peers as well as his or her
boss and subordinates.

4. A manager's method of fulfilling accountability can vary,   85
subject to the individual's style, but common management principles should prevail within an organization.

5. A manager's effectiveness is not determined by job know-how   87
or education. Management, a profession unto itself, requires
enduring and cohesive drill in the management process by all
managers, at all levels.

6. Managers can be moved from one function to another. A   91
manager must have the ability to take over a number of diverse
activities.

7. A manager must preserve detached and nonpersonal relation-   93
ships throughout the organization.

8. Success as a manager depends upon the manager's ability to   94
develop and utilize available resources. To maximize the use of
others is a full-time occupation.

THE ROLE OF THE MANAGER (CONT.)   Page Ref.

9. The true value of a manager is determined by his or her contri-   95
bution to the success of others.

10. An organization should make the criteria for manager selec-   96
tion, evaluation, development, and promotion common knowledge.
The measurements should be known.

MANAGER CRITERIA   Page Ref.

Manager criteria should be based on the specific needs of the   103
organization as well as the demands of the management function.
They could include, but not be limited to, the following:

A. Wants and likes position   104
    1. accepts accountability

B. Has strong sense of self; self-confident   104
    1. possesses presence
    2. able to act and to stand alone
    3. does not need authority
    4. tells others what to do
    5. benefits from criticism
    6. admits personal deficiencies
    7. learns from others
    8. works with a quality of ignorance and intelligent ineffective-
ness

C. Team player   108
    1. thinks and acts organizationally
    2. activates employee development
    3. corrects malpractices personally
    4. gains satisfaction from subordinate success

D. Possesses conscience or sense of internalized moral standards   110

LINE RELATIONSHIPS   Page Ref.

A **line relationship** is that direct, unbroken one between any   113
individual and his or her immediate superior or his or her immediate
subordinates, if any.

1. Under all circumstances within the structure, each person has   115
only one boss represented by the immediate reporting relationship.

2. The effectiveness of the line relationship is dependent on   116
whether the individuals concerned practice what is necessary to
keep it healthy.

3. In a manager-to-specialist (boss/subordinate) relationship, the   117
line relationship becomes the basis around which to delegate
responsibility, to set performance standards, and to evaluate
performance.

4. In a manager-to-manager (boss/subordinate) relationship, the   117
line relationship becomes the basis around which to define and
accept accountability and to recognize performance.

5. The line relationship does not limit the manager's freedom to   118
use staff relationships.

STAFF RELATIONSHIPS

A **staff relationship** is any relationship between managers which is
not a line relationship. Staff relationships are used to help a manager fulfill his or her accountability; they constitute the managerial
network of an organization.

1. A staff relationship is used to introduce proposals to any
management sector and to employ constructive means to cause
acceptance of those proposals.

2. The staff relationship can be initiated by any manager. When
employing a staff relationship, the manager must respect line
relationships and act in accordance with organizational goals
(organizational accountability).

3. The manager employing a staff relationship to make proposals
is not accountable for the acceptance or implementation of his or
her proposals.

4. Whether or not inputs provided through staff relationships are
accepted is determined by the accountable manager receiving the
inputs.

5. Given healthy line relationships, staff relationships are the
ingredient that enables an organization to function smoothly and
effectively.

THE ROLE OF THE SPECIALIST   Page Ref.

A **specialist** is the receiver of and fulfiller of specific responsibilities   133
as delegated by his or her manager.

1. The specialist must fulfill his or her work assignment.   136

2. The specialist must recognize the manager as the person who   136
provides direction and assistance in fulfilling the specialist's work
assignment.

3. The specialist must recognize the manager's accountability for   136
what happens in the specific work area.

4. The specialist must recognize that the manager might designate   139
certain qualified personnel (manager or specialist) to assist the
specialist in the accomplishment of the specialist's job.

5. The specialist must appreciate and accept that decisions are   139
made for the common organizational good.

6. The specialist must have the freedom to contact other manage-   140
rial personnel as required by his or her job assignment or as an alternate line of communication regarding his or her employment
status.

THE MANAGER-TO-SPECIALIST RELATIONSHIP

THE MANAGER-TO-MANAGER RELATIONSHIP   Page Ref.

Rules Governing the Manager (boss)-to-Manager (subordinate) line relationship at all levels:

MANAGER DEVELOPMENT Page Ref.

Although the manager's position is a dynamic one and personal 167
provision must be made for self-development, there should be
organizational disciplines designed to address the essential requirements of the management operation. Manager development can
include, but is not limited to:

A. The Job: 168
1. position descriptions
2. performance standards
3. evaluation systems
4. wage and salary structures
5. boss/subordinate relationships

B. The Organization: 169
1. staff meetings
2. organization models
3. fixed manager criteria
4. skill inventories
5. management training

C. The Experience: 171
1. special assignments
2. experience exchanges

D. The Opportunity: 172
1. promotion from within

1. An organization can never cause anyone to become a manager. 172
Assistance and opportunity for such progression can be afforded,
but the desire, effort, and accountability for betterment as a
manager must be within the person concerned.